A Concise Guide to the ARTILLERY AT GETTYSBURG

D1562646

Gregory A. Coco

Savas Beatie
California

Library of Congress Control Number: 2022939347

First Savas Beatie Edition, First Printing

ISBN-13: 978-1-61121-651-6
eISBN: 978-1-954547-53-7 (Savas Publishing)

SB

Savas Beatie
989 Governor Drive, Suite 102
El Dorado Hills, CA 95762
916-941-6896
www.savasbeatie.com
sales@savasbeatie.com

Savas Beatie titles are available at special discounts for bulk purchases by corporations, institutions, and others. For more details, please contact contact us at sales@savasbeatie.com or visit www.savasbeatie.com for more information.

This special edition is dedicated to the memory of

Alcide H. Normand,

a former Confederate artilleryman, and veteran of
the Siege of Port Hudson and other battles.

He raised my grandfather Edward A. Coco as his own son, from 1876 to 1895,
thereby obtaining forever an honored place in our family history.

THE
GREGORY A. COCO
COLLECTION

by Savas Beatie

TABLE OF CONTENTS

Acknowledgments

In particular I would like to recognize Civil War veteran James K.P. Scott, whose manuscript on the artillery at Gettysburg formed the incentive and outline for a large portion of this project. Although heavily paraphrased, the heart of his narrative was retained. My gratitude is also extended to the following people who made this book possible and at the same time enhanced its style and content: To Cindy L. Small, for typing, editing, proofreading, and general assistance, and for her constant companionship, love, and encouragement. Dean S. Thomas, for twenty years of friendship and business cooperation. Licensed Battlefield Guides Anthony J. Kelly and James M. Clouse for editorial advice and comments, all of which improved this publication substantially. Lynn W. Myers for the excellent artwork and cartography herein, Steven C. Hollingshead for his usual fine photography, and Darrell L. Smoker and Dwight Van Nitz for research services. And finally to the staff at Thomas Publications for their attention to detail and for the high quality of editing, design, layout, marketing, advertising and production for the first edition of this work: Sarah S. Rodgers, James E. Thomas, Thomas A. Desjardin, Barbara L. Grant and Scott E. Wolf. And now in 2007, appreciation and thanks go to long time friend Phil Cole for his interest and dedication in bringing back my artillery handbook into a second edition.

My thanks and appreciation to you all.

Gregory A. Coco
Gettysburg, PA
December 4, 2007

Introduction

Within but a day or two following the departure of the Army of the Potomac and the Army of Northern Virginia from the battlefields surrounding Gettysburg, an inexperienced militia regiment arrived on the scene. This unit was sent from the capital at Harrisburg, just 35 miles to the north, to gather in the injured and stragglers from both armies, secure the useable weapons and equipment left on the field, and transport the wounded as fast as their condition would permit. This nearly thousand-man force, called the 36th Pennsylvania Emergency Militia, was commanded by Col. Henry C. Alleman. Eventually, in the weeks subsequent to the great battle, it collected and sent away 12,061 wounded Union soldiers and 6,197 Confederates; it also picked up 26,664 muskets, 9,250 bayonets, 14,000 rounds of small-arms ammunition, and almost 50 wagon loads of clothing and equipment, along with thousands of other discarded accouterments.   But in that entire 25 square mile area comprising the Gettysburg battleground, Alleman could not report finding even one cannon left behind by the two armies. Considering the fact that over 630 of these weapons had been brought along on the campaign and were heavily engaged for three days of very severe combat, Alleman's disclosure is a surprising revelation. However, such was the respect and regard for the artillery, that rarely was a serviceable piece ever abandoned by an army if it could in any way be retained.[1]

In the mountains of manuscript sources available to the researchers of the American Civil War, countless reports, letters, diaries, and memoirs attest to the fascination the artillery held for officers and enlisted men alike.   Whether or not that arm of the military actually made any great difference in the outcome of over 10,000 battles, sieges, or skirmishes between 1861 and 1865, appears to be almost irrelevant to the participants.   Frankly, the influence generated by the ominous looking cannons that accompanied the armies, and their real or perceived aura of importance, power, invincibility and strength, was a serious factor that could and cannot be ignored.   The surviving documentation of that conflict is replete with quotes concerning the near majesty of the artillery in battle. Most personal narratives, when speaking of the subject, read a lot like this portrayal, which was composed by Pvt. Edward W. Spangler, 130th Pennsylvania Infantry, of a scene during the Battle of Antietam:

When we began our march for the battle line, about 8 A. M., a battalion of artillery with guns at full gallop swept into position, opening in volleys. It was a grand and inspiring sight to witness batteries going headlong into action, – the neighing of horses, the rumbling of caissons, the halt, the furious cannonade, the officers on their chargers with swords gleaming in the sunlight, with buglers clanging out the order, the passing of ammunition, the ramming, the sighting, the firing, and the swabbing, – the guns booming in chorus like heaven-rending thunder.[2]

The artillerymen themselves were, in turn, justly proud of their own contributions, yet they often only wrote of the mechanics or "science," of that branch of the army. This is apparent in a letter written home by Pvt. Arthur A. Blandin. In it, he boasted to his family that his Massachusetts battery could limber up, trot to a position two-and-a-half miles away, go into action, and fire its rounds in just 44 minutes. Blandin also explained that in shooting at a target made of poles and green paper one mile away, his gun crew could hit it with a 20-pounder Parrott shell on the fourth try. He added:

> It takes 6 seconds for a shell to go 1 mile. We have fuzes that we put into the shell when we fire one & we have to judge how far the distance so as to know how long a fuse to put into the shell to have it burst when it strikes. The elevation of the gun to fire 1 mile is 4.5 degrees for a Schenkl shell & 4.25 deg. for a Hotchkiss shell....[3]

Invariably though, battle narratives were the meat and potatoes of almost any good wartime story. Facing or firing the guns, it seems, made for the ultimate exciting reminiscence left by soldiers North and South. Scores of them sounded much like this one:

> Waiting till they were breast high, my battery was discharged at them, every gun loaded... with double shotted canister and solid shot, after which through the smoke [we] caught a glimpse of the enemy, they were torn and broken, but still advancing....
> The enemy [then] crowded to the very muzzles of [our guns] but were blown away by the canister. Sergeant after Sergt. was struck down, horses were plunging and laying about all around, bullets now came in on all sides, for the enemy had turned our flank. The air was dark with smoke....The enemy were yelling like

demons....

    [W]e fought with our guns untill the rebs could put their hands on [them]...the bullets flew thick as hailstones, it is a wonder we were not all killed...not a man run, [sic] 4 or 5 fell within 15 feet of me....[4]

Often soldiers expressed horror and astonishment at the cruel or humorous antics of a projectile, such as shown in this account by Sgt. Frank H. Venn, 19th Mississippi Infantry:

    We were all lying low [on the battlefield of Antietam] when it came hurling towards us with a searching sound, alighting at the head of our line, recoiling repeatedly in its course, but each time missing a man. At the lower end, [of our position] away to the left, a man had his back turned in the direction whence the missile came, but, fortunately, by the time it reached him its force was spent, and falling by its own weight, it gave him a final tap on the back of his cranium, - a gentle reminder to wake up, – but inflicting no wound. [5]

Being under direct fire from an iron-spitting battery during an infantry attack was no picnic either, as the words of Lt. Edgar A. Burpee, 19th Maine, written soon after the Battle of Gettysburg, attest:

    It was a trying moment when...we rose up to breast the storm...from the enemies' guns. The men dropped so fast...but the thought of retreating never occurred to me...when we charged down the hill..,though shot and shell and grape was coming like a hurricane....You cannot conceive the terrible shriek and noise of shell and appalling report grape and canister make when it strikes the ground. It almost makes a man shudder and cringe to be a listener to it. It requires much strength of mind to compose oneself when lying under a rapid shelling....[6]

There are too, countless history pages devoted to the aftermath of war and the unmitigated havoc, death, and destruction inflicted by artillery rounds. These sad and pathetic reminders of close combat were present on all battlefields where cannons were fired point blank into massed human ranks. In one article completed more than 20 years after the war, Gettysburg native John Howard Wert, was still able to precisely describe a wretched location he had visited in 1863 on a piece of the bitterly contested turf at Gettysburg:

The scenes of that spot...still linger on our memories.... Masses of [infantry] advanced up to the muzzles of [the] guns, which had been loaded either with double shotted canister or spherical case, with fuzes cut to one second – to explode near the muzzles – [and] had been litterally blown to atoms – and in a moment's brief space into eternity. Corpses strewed the ground at every step. Arms, legs, heads, and parts of dismembered bodies were scattered all about, and sticking among the rocks, and against the trunks of trees, hair, brains, entrails, and shreds of human flesh still hung, a disgusting, sickening, heartrending spectacle to our young minds. It was indeed a charnel house - a butcher's pen - with man as the victim.[7]

It has been sometimes noted by historians who were critical of the tactical significance of the artillery, that its "bark was worse than its bite." This view is partially accurate, as cannon fire in the majority of Civil War engagements accounted for a small total of the overall casualties, usually between one and 10 percent. One veteran who formed this impression was Surgeon Henry Janes of the 3rd Vermont Infantry. He was the Union officer left behind in charge of 21,000 wounded soldiers following the Battle of Gettysburg. In an 1899 letter published by a Baltimore newspaper, Dr. Janes outlined these interesting observations:

The proportion of cases in which artillerymen are able in the excitement of battle, to burst shells in exactly the right position in front of a line of battle to do much execution is very small, even at a range of only one mile. At a distance of two miles or more, the risk to the men in a moving skirmish line is hardly entitled to the classification of "extra hazardous" by the insurance underwriters.

The execution done by the artillery in battle is usually greatly overrated. During our Civil War, out of 245,790 shot wounds [to Federal soldiers] 14,032 were caused by artillery, viz, 350 by solid shot, 12,520 by fragments of shells, etc., and 1,153 by grape and canister....

Just before Pickett's celebrated charge at Gettysburg the Confederates opened upon our line with about 150 pieces of artillery, which were immediately answered by an equal [number] on our side, but among the 20,995 Union and Confederate wounded left under the charge of the writer on this battlefield there were only 204 wounds caused by artillery. On [many other] occasions the writer was in position to know definitely the number injured by artillery, [when] the firing was at short range and under unusually favorable circumstances for effectiveness....[8]

Nonetheless, in more than a few battles and skirmishes, injuries and deaths caused by shot, shell, and canister may have raised these calculations somewhat higher. And perhaps, Dr. Janes and others ignored the possibility that wounds from the case shot or shrapnel balls of artillery rounds so resembled those of .69 caliber musket balls as to be undetectable, or that the solid or exploding projectiles performed their deadly business so well that only corpses remained behind to tell few tales to statisticians figuring out such tragic computations. But physical losses alone are not what made the artillery a potent offensive or defensive weapon. The sound, sight or even mere presence of a gun battery of dull glinting bronze, or black-painted iron, could in fact, be counted on to produce a deep impression on any troops in their presence, especially if that presence meant exposure to their bite.

Arguably, the fundamental psychological effect alone was very likely worth the cost of keeping the expense of artillery, present and equipped, within the armies. However, the potential real value of this service arm may not have been grasped by a large number of commanders during the four-year-long conflict. As a general rule, during most battles, artillery units were piecemealed out to individual infantry brigades, thereby wasting not only a higher material damage effect, but also by reducing the mental shock and other subconscious advantages they held as well.

Two young artillerymen. Pvt.Charlie Camm of the 1ˢᵗ Co., Richmond Howitzers, CSA (left), and an unknown Yankee (right).

To be deployed effectively, artillery batteries had to be concentrated in dominating clusters on key terrain features, so as to mass their overwhelming weight of fire against a particular or isolated target. And secondly, by arranging guns in heavy enfilading crossfires, a more destructive result could be effected than simply by direct, frontal fire. At the same time, this maneuver relieved the gunners from the fear of being overrun by enemy troops. The problems of difficult terrain aside, when substantial numbers of cannon were assembled in such a manner, they could sway the course and outcome of a battle significantly. Therefore, if one army could establish its "grand battery" at the right location before the enemy arrived, it could, in theory, dismount their guns faster than they could come on line and return fire. Also, massed artillery might shatter infantry columns before they could attack. By forcing the opposing troops to seek cover, they were eliminated from assembling their own artillery, or using their infantry effectively.

Customarily, Civil War cannon were considered to be of superior value chiefly in defensive functions, and it was in this feature that they excelled. Long-range, focused bombardments, where the targets were mostly invisible, usually proved inadequate in providing support for a ground attack. To search out and destroy the enemy's batteries and infantry regiments by this modern day method, was, due to the simple weapons and the limitations of fire control, clearly difficult and nearly impossible, unless, of course, the intended targets were left exposed. But, on the other hand, placed in weighty concentrations along or within an infantry line of battle, batteries always stiffened and strengthened such a formation. And at short, deadly distances, the guns often broke up an assaulting force at distances between 1,000 yards down to less than 100 feet. An astute officer could use the sinister power of the cannon to impress and intimidate his enemy into forgoing an attack altogether.

Detractors have stated that artillery's ability to act in defense was overshadowed by its vulnerability to long-distance infantry musketry fire, all due to pre-war improvements in the range and accuracy of rifles. This belief is also misleading in many respects, mainly because of the documented frequent and precise use of field pieces at distances of less than 1,000 yards. At these ranges and less, cannons had a positive tactical effect on squads of infantrymen, (whose weapons were usually ineffective over 300 yards) attempting to knock out gun crews; they habitually smothered most small arms fire before it could seriously hurt the battery's performance. Time and time again, casualty figures have proven that even after batteries had engaged riflemen for long periods of time, there were relatively few deaths and injuries accumulated in these units. In the end, enough men usually remained upright to handle the pieces, since, on an average, most battery captains kept between 17 and 25 men trained per gun. Hence a command consisting of 100 to 125 members, might lose five men to long-range cannonading or counter-battery fire, and five more to musketry, but would still retain from seven to 15 individuals for each piece. So the genuine threat to a battery in battle was not "sharpshooters," but regular foot soldiers advancing to within 30 and 100 yards, a fairly rare occasion, especially if the artillerymen were supported by nearby friendly troops.

Another important point in evaluating Civil War artillery was its proficiency, or lack thereof, in the art of supporting infantry directly in an attack, or what is sometimes known as the "artillery charge." Unfortunately, ineffective long-range fire was about the only assistance batteries could normally provide to an infantry force, as in the critical cannonade generated prior to Gen. James Longstreet's 12,000-man assault at Gettysburg on July 3. Truthfully, in following up an infantry attack, a surging counter-stroke by horse-drawn artillery was exceedingly rare. Such was the exact case though, on July 2, when a group of Confederate First Corps batteries charged forward toward the abandoned Federal line at the "Peach Orchard" and Emmitsburg Road. The usefulness of the "artillery charge" was, at Gettysburg, as on most occasions, not proven to show substantial or practical benefits.

Despite many shortcomings and an often misunderstanding of its versatility and best uses, artillery did play a crucial role in many Civil War battles, and was even positively decisive in some. It could never be ignored, and commanders were wise not to think cannon might be rendered obsolete purely by a measured progress in the development of better military small arms. In fact, it can be proven that the trend was moving the other way. In the eastern U.S. armies, for instance, the ratio of field guns to infantry increased between the years 1862-1865, from two-and-a-half cannon per 1,000 men in the Army of the Potomac, to three or four per thousand.

In battle an artillery battery on line covered 82 yards, with 14-17 yards between guns, and a nine-man crew per piece. On the march, batteries traveled in single file covering two-and-one-half miles per hour. At a rapid march, five miles-per-hour could be attained, but only for short distances. Under excellent conditions a battery pulled by its 90+ horses might move 35-40 miles per day.

In the Confederate Army of Northern Virginia, despite material shortages, there was even a better relationship; that force often fielded four guns per thousand and sometimes reached seven, nine, or even 10 per 1,000. As one historian observed: "Artillery can scarcely have been an irrelevance on the Civil War battlefield if so shrewd a commander as Robert E. Lee habitually accepted such a disproportionately heavy train of guns in his army."[9]

A Narrative of the Artillery in the Battle at Gettysburg

The Army of the Potomac

The splendid record made by the field artillery of the United States Army in the war with Mexico in 1846-47 was followed by a period of almost total disregard by the War Department, which almost immediately dismounted three-fourths of its authorized batteries. In 1861, provision was made for the reorganization and command of the artillery in the field, but it was left without a head; its control and direction subject to the personal whims of the various army commanders. Field officers were considered an unnecessary expense and their muster into service forbidden. Batteries in service were often dependent on the accompanying infantry for their support for men enough to work the guns; horses were supplied, but usually after the ambulance and quartermaster's trains had been provided for. In spite of this official enmity, many a hard-fought field attests to the courage and self-sacrifice of officers and men. It was no unusual sight to find, after the close of a battle, the officer in command of a battery dead at the guns he served. As the grade of captain seemed to be the limit of promotion, many able artillerists sought transfer to other arms of the service.

When the Army of the Potomac was organized, a strong artillery arm was formed, with one-third of the artillery posted as a reserve, and the other two-thirds distributed among the infantry divisions – one regular battery and three volunteer batteries to a division. Under this organization, Maj. William F. Barry of the 5th U.S. Artillery was commissioned brigadier general and made Chief of Artillery. Major Henry J. Hunt, also in the 5th U.S. Artillery, was commissioned colonel and put in command of the reserve. On September 5, 1862 Barry was assigned to be Inspector General of Artillery for the whole army, Col. Hunt then succeeded him as Chief of Artillery for the Army of the Potomac, with the rank of brigadier general of volunteers.

Some months earlier on or about June 1, 1862, a new reorganization had taken one-half of the artillery from the infantry divisions and formed these units into a reserve for each corps, the command of which was given to officers designated by the corps commanders.

During the Antietam Campaign, recently promoted Brigadier General Hunt found himself, two days before that battle, in absolute control of the entire artillery force with full power to use the name of the commanding general whenever he came in contact with an officer superior in rank to himself. Partly due to this new situation, the artillery arm acquitted itself in an admirable manner on that bloody field, where its record still speaks for itself.

When Gen. Joseph Hooker relieved Gen. Ambrose E. Burnside, Gen. Hunt received orders inconsistent with his former position under Generals George B. McClellan and Burnside. Hunt was once again delegated into an administrative role in which the duties of "combat commander" were removed from his list of responsibilities. Gen. Hunt rightfully complained of this irregular separation of the command and administration obligations in the artillery of the Army of the Potomac, but this frustrating problem continued to trouble him until just before the Gettysburg Campaign.

At the beginning of the Chancellorsville Campaign there were over 400 guns in the Potomac army plus all artillery carriages and ammunition trains, accompanied by 8,000 or 9,000 horses and 10,000 men. This, in strength and importance to the military, was actually an army corps and should have had as its chief a major general with adequate brigadier generals and field-officers, and a full and complete staff. Incredibly, this arm of the service, the equivalent of an army corps, was commanded only by a brigadier general, and, including himself, there were but six officers above the grade of captain. Imagine if you will what would have happened to the First Corps at Gettysburg with but one brigadier and five field officers present on July 1-3.

While at Frederick, MD, on June 28, 1863, with Gen. George G. Meade the newly appointed head of the Army of the Potomac, Gen. Hunt resumed full control of the artillery of that army. In this campaign there were 67 batteries present (between 358 and 372 guns), with over 7,900 men and 8,400 horses, and the usual complement of material and ammunition trains. During the

General Henry Hunt

15

Battle of Gettysburg nearly 370 guns were distributed among 65 batteries; about 212 guns with the infantry, 50 with the cavalry, and 108 consigned to the artillery reserve. Two batteries of 4.5-inch rifles (B & M, 1st CT) had been left at Westminster, MD.

The 212 or so guns assigned to the infantry were distributed, approximately, in brigades of five six-gun batteries to each of the seven infantry corps. These brigades were commanded by two colonels, one major, three captains, and one lieutenant. The 50 guns assigned to the cavalry were in two brigades of five and four-gun batteries overseen by captains. The 108 guns of the artillery reserve were in five brigades (four, four-gun batteries and one of five) commanded by one lieutenant colonel and four captains. Gen. Robert O. Tyler led the reserve.

Arriving on the field of Gettysburg, Gen. Hunt was again able to exercise all of the duties as commander of the artillery as recognized in modern armies of the time. He was at every point of attack and, when necessary, brought up batteries from an adjoining corps or from the artillery reserve; in fact, he gave every order found essential under the circumstances.

It is not within the limits of this chapter to give in detail the entire battle history of each and every artillery unit at Gettysburg. Therefore, within the space available, from a selection of the 65 batteries present on the field, some notable examples of artillery work will be explored.

The First Corps

Arguably, beginning with the first day at Gettysburg, every Federal battery engaged could be seen as a "notable example." Capt. James H. Cooper (B, 1st PA), Capt. Gilbert H. Reynolds (L, 1st NY), and Capt. Greenleaf T. Stevens (E, 5th ME) fought all day and never better than at the end of July 1 when they made a final stand at the Lutheran Theological Seminary. Captain John A. Calef, (A, 2nd US) followed by Capt. James A. Hall, (B, 2nd ME) began the fight; the former firing the first cannon-shot of the Army of the Potomac, the latter engaged until compelled to abandon his position and one of his guns, which was later recovered. Lieutenant James Stewart (B, 4th US), whose battery was known throughout the war as always being where it was most needed, is entitled to special notice; on Wednesday July 1 he was in the right place at the right time. General James S. Wadsworth in his official report says of this battery: "Lieutenant Stewart came to our assistance and rendered effective service demolishing a brigade of the enemy by a destructive fire of canister and shell." The battery was posted on both sides of a railroad cut through Oak Ridge; the right section of guns on the north side under Lieutenant Stewart engaged and held back Gen. Junius Daniel's North Carolina Brigade. The left, under Lt. James Davison, was on the south side of the cut. Davison swung his guns around to enfilade, at 100 yards, Gen. Alfred M. Scales' North Carolina brigade then advancing over the space between the Edward McPherson buildings and the Seminary. General Scales was wounded by this fire, and every field officer of his brigade but one was put out of action during this part of the fight. Major General William D. Pender, the division commander, was slightly wounded while rallying Scales' brigade. Stewart's battery, pressed by Confederates on its front and flanks, retired from the ridge and passed through the town to East Cemetery Hill. It sustained a loss of 36. (Stewart and Davison were both among the wounded). It can be said that the spirited and aggressive work of the First Corps' batteries contributed materially to the selection of the battlefields and positions of the Union army for the second and third days' combat.

Position of Stewart's Battery B (4th US) looking toward the terrain of the first day's action at the "railroad cut" north of the Chambersburg Road.

The Eleventh Corps

The artillery units of the Eleventh Corps did all that could possibly be expected of them, given the poor defensive terrain they were compelled by circumstances to select. Lieutenant Bayard Wilkeson (G, 4th US) was cut down near Blocher's hill, now called Barlow Knoll, on the Harrisburg Road and carried just to the rear. He died there at the county almshouse, where he was later buried by his father, a news reporter covering the Army of the Potomac. Captain Hubert Dilger (I, 1st OH) severely damaged the Southern troops and guns opposed to him, and in one instance plugged the muzzle of an enemy Napoleon with one of his unit's 12-pound cannon balls. When compelled to retire, he made a stand along the Mummasburg Road, and then afterward unlimbered a section in the town square. Captain Lewis Heckman, (K, 1st OH) was in action only 30 minutes but lost two men killed, one officer and 10 men wounded, and two men missing, plus nine horses killed. He expended 113 rounds, mostly canister, and retired through Gettysburg's streets leaving one of his guns to the bayonets of the enemy. Captain Michael Wiedrich, (I, 1st NY) posted on East Cemetery Hill, halted Gen. Robert F. Hoke's North Carolina brigade (led by Col. Isaac E. Avery) in the flat ground east of the town, and took part the next day in a duel with Gen. Richard S. Ewell's artillery on Benner's Hill.

One of Lt. Wilkeson's cannon, (G, 4th US), on Blocher's Hill is aimed toward Jones' Confederate battalion position a mile away across Rock Creek.

A 3-inch Ordnance Rifle of Wheeler's 13th New York Battery faces
Southern guns on Oak Hill

The cannons which had pulled back during the retreat of the First and Eleventh Corps were posted at the end of the battle's first day on the Cemetery hills and McKnight's hill, or what is now known as Stevens Knoll. Of the First Corps batteries, 83 officers and men were killed and wounded, including Capt. Stevens and Lt. Charles O. Hunt. Capt. Reynolds, Lt. Stewart, Lt. Davison and Lt. William C. Miller, were also among the injured. A large loss in horses (80) occurred between Seminary Ridge and the town when they were subjected to enemy fire from the rear and both flanks. This fire felled the horses from one of Reynold's pieces causing it to be left on the field.

The Eleventh Corps batteries had 69 officers and men killed, wounded and missing, including Lt. Wilkeson. There were 98 horses left dead and two guns abandoned, one from Heckman's and another from Lt. William Wheeler's (13th NY); the latter was recovered when the Confederate army retreated.

The Second Corps

The artillery brigade was favored above its fellows by opportunity; Lt. George A. Woodruff, (I, 1st US), Capt. William A. Arnold, (A, 1st RI), Lt. T. Fred Brown, (B, 1st RI), Lt. Alonzo H. Cushing, (A, 4th US), and Capt. James M. Rorty, (B, 1st NY), all saw heavy action. During the forenoon of the third day, Lt. Woodruff had eight separate engagements with the enemy's cannon, and was mortally wounded during the period covered by the Pickett-Pettigrew charge. Lieutenant Cushing was killed, and Lt. Joseph S. Milne who was temporarily attached to his battery, was mortally injured at the Angle on Cemetery Ridge, an area formed by a 90-degree turn in a stone wall on the farm of Peter Frey. Captain Rorty died near there too, and Lt. Albert S. Sheldon was wounded. Lieutenant Brown was severely wounded in the neck by a musket ball. At sunset on July 2 the guns of Arnold, Cushing, and Brown were temporarily overrun by Confederate infantry, but were recaptured and again in the fight the following day. On that final afternoon of the battle, Cushing and his batterymen were the focus of attention at the Angle, and it was there that he lost his life. In addition, Lt. Milne was mortally wounded, Lt. Samuel Canby severely wounded, and five of Cushing's men were killed and 31 injured. Cushing was hit twice before he received the last bullet. Woodruff fell at the moment of victory, with Lt. Tully McCrea succeeding to the command of the battery survivors. Captain Rorty had joined his battery on the afternoon of the second day only to lose his life July 3. So great was the loss of this brigade in officers and men that Woodruff's and Cushing's batteries, and Arnold's and Brown's batteries were consolidated. Woodruff died July 4, and, at his own request, was buried on the field where he shed his blood for his country. Colonel Francis E. Pierce, 108th New York, called him the bravest man he ever saw in combat.

The Third Corps

General Daniel E. Sickles' unauthorized forward movement of the Third Corps on July 2 brought all manner of trouble to the artillery brigade attached to his corps, and to others. Captain James E. Smith, (4th NY) traded three of his guns at Devil's Den to the First Texas and the Fifteenth Georgia for time; these cannon were not recovered until Appomattox. Captain George B. Winslow, (D, 1st NY) held a bad position in John Rose's wheat field. With the enemy in the woods on two sides within musket range he was compelled to retire, which he did piece by piece. Captain A. Judson Clark, (B, 1st NJ) and Lt. John K. Bucklyn, (E, 1st RI) were near Joseph Sherfy's peach orchard, one on each wing of an angle with the apex at the orchard. These batteries were compelled to retreat amid their infantry support, when the Federal line was broken at

A view from the Peach Orchard toward the ground covered by McLaws' Division attack of July 2.

Sherfy's farm buildings across and along the Emmitsburg Road. Lieutenant Francis W. Seeley, (K, 4th US), was first on the north then on the south side of the David Klingel house further up that same road. About 5:30 P.M. Lt. Seeley was grievously wounded and the battery under Lt. Robert James remained under a punishing musketry fire after their infantry protection fell back. The battery was then withdrawn, but later formed part of a new line of guns gathered by Lt. Col. Freeman McGilvery east of Plum Run and north of George Weikert's small stone farmhouse. Captain George E. Randolph, who commanded the artillery brigade, was wounded early in the action, and was succeeded by Capt. Clark. Lieutenant Bucklyn, of Randolph's old battery, received a painful wound from Rebel fire.

During the Battle of Gettysburg well over 55,000 artillery projectiles were fired by both armies. Generally each cannon crew had available 200 rounds of ammunition present for its piece. Another 250 rounds per gun were required to be present in the ordnance supply wagons accompanying the army. These vehicles had a red six-inch horizontal stripe painted on the canvas covers, as well as the division and corps number it belonged to.

The Fifth Corps

The Fifth Corps artillery entered the fray between 4 and 5 P.M. on July 2. Lieutenant Charles E. Hazlett, (D, 5th US), Lt. Aaron F. Walcott, (C, 3rd MA), and Lt. Malbone F. Watson, (I, 5th US) were positioned in rear of Gen. James Barnes' Division; Capt. Frank C. Gibbs, (L, 1st OH), and Capt. Almont Barnes, (C, 1st NY) supported Gen. Romeyn B. Ayres' Division. Watson and Walcott were intercepted by an aide of Gen. Sickles who commandeered their guns to help remedy the Third Corps' defective placement, thus depriving the Fifth Corps of two-fifths of its firepower. At 5:30 Watson was sent forward to the Peach Orchard to relieve Capt. Nelson Ames, (G, 1st NY) of the artillery reserve. Hazlett's Battery, meanwhile, had been moved over to the left and gained a strong position on the crest of Little Round Top. Lieutenant Hazlett was killed on this lofty site and was immediately succeeded by Lt. Benjamin F. Rittenhouse, under whose direction the rifled guns were professionally served against Gen. George Pickett's lines the next day. When Lt. Watson was wounded, control of his battery came under the authority of Lt. Charles C. MacConnell, who abandoned the ground at the Peach Orchard and regrouped about 350 yards eastward across the marshy banks of Plum Run where his unit lacked support of any kind. Here, the 21st Mississippi, one of Gen. William Barksdale's regiments, swarmed into Battery I driving the gunners away at the point of the bayonet. MacConnell's remaining officers and men fell back until they encountered the 39th New York Infantry which had been posted to protect the flank of Col. George L. Willard's brigade then in conflict with Barksdale. There Lt. Samuel Peeples of the battery picked up a musket and led the 39th in recapturing the guns.

The Sixth Corps

Eight batteries made up the artillery brigade of the Sixth Corps. On the afternoon of July 3 they were parked in the fields east of the Taneytown Road and the Round Tops. With the exception of Capt. Andrew Cowan, (1st NY) none of them were engaged. Capt. William H. McCartney, (A, 1st MA), Capt. William A. Harn, (3rd NY) were moved to Cemetery Hill; Lt. John A. Butler, (G, 2nd US), and Lt. Leonard Martin, (F, 5th US) were directed to David Zeigler's woods on the north end of Cemetery Ridge at the conclusion of Gen. James Longstreet's assault that same day.

Captain Cowan and the officers and men of his battery deserve special mention for the many post-war years of patience with which they heard the efficient services of their battery commended by historians and in the official reports credited, through some error, to another unit, Lt. William Wheeler's 13th New York. Later stories established Cowan with having relieved Lt. Thomas F. Brown, (B, 1st RI) at the clump of trees at the end of the third day's artillery duel, when, in fact, he was in action on the ridge from the beginning. Even Gen. Henry Hunt in his report brackets him with Capt. Robert H. Fitzhugh's (K, 1st NY), Lt. Augustin N. Parsons' (A, 1st NJ) and Lt. Gulian V. Weir's (C, 5th US), bringing them in at 3:00 P.M.

About mid-day on Friday July 3, Capt. Cowan was ordered to report his battery to Gen. John Newton of the First Corps. Preceding his unit, Cowan came onto the field in search of Newton. He met Gen. Abner Doubleday, one of the division commanders, who informed him that Gen. Newton was out on the line and that he, Doubleday, would take his report. From where they stood they could see the sun's reflection from some of Confederate Col. Edward P. Alexander's bronze pieces in position near and at the Peach Orchard. General Doubleday thought they would not be able to use his (Cowan's) battery at that point as it would draw a return fire that would cause unnecessary loss to the infantrymen massed in their rear. The captain therefore was directed to park in the fields east of the Taneytown Road near the Granite Schoolhouse Road intersection. The New Yorker rested his battery as directed, saw Gen. Newton, reported his location and was in the act of stretching himself on the ground for some much-needed sleep when Alexander's opening chorus began, throwing a multitude of Rebel missiles into the air overhead, but happily, twenty-five feet too high for damage. The battery was at once assembled and took the Taneytown Road towards Cemetery Hill. Somewhere just north of Nicholas Codori's spring, Capt. Cowan rode to the crest of Cemetery Ridge, estimated the proper direction and range and ordered up his battery, leaving the caissons in the rear. He came into position with Doubleday's division, and Capt. James Rorty, (B, 1st NY), the next battery on his right. Cowan opened at once with his 3-inch rifles presenting a slow, accurate fire against the enemy guns in front. When the infantry assault developed, he observed a general officer in rear of the Angle area waving his sword with a motion interpreted to mean bring his battery to the right. The captain obeyed the order and discovered it came from Gen. Alexander S. Webb who led the Second Brigade, Second Division, Second Corps. He limbered to the right at a gallop and came

Captain Cowan's 1ˢᵗ New York Battery stood near this position at one time on July 3. Pickett's Division advanced through the Nicholas Codori farm seen above the gun.

into position between Rorty and Lt. Cushing who was then supplementing Brown's Rhode Islander's diminishing firepower. Cowan's right piece was carried by its impetus until, when halted, it was in Cushing's domain; therefore, he asked Cushing to look after this gun. The other five pieces were engaged south of a line marked by a clump of trees just to the southeast of the famous angle in the stone wall, the right piece a few yards where the battery monument now stands. There was a regiment of infantry behind a slight defense of rails forward of these five ordnance rifles. When Gen. Lewis A. Armistead's troops of Pickett's Division entered the ground within the Angle, these riflemen were pulled from Cowan's field of fire and to his right by Gen. Webb. This uncovered Cowan's artillerymen to a body of Armistead's men who had halted at a rocky outcropping some fifty yards westward out toward the Codori farmhouse. With a shout of "Come on Boys, get those guns," they charged right into the face of a tempest of double canister that almost swept them from Cowan's front. Some of them, however, succeeded in passing the slight breast-work. One gallant young man, a Virginia officer, was foremost to the battery when he was literally torn to pieces by the blast that followed the firing of several 3-inch rifles at less than fifty feet. When Pickett's men were turned back, Arnold, Cushing and Rorty having withdrawn, Cowan's were the only guns remaining in the area. Following behind Pickett's forces, Col. Alexander had advanced several smoothbore cannons to the Emmitsburg Road. Cowan concentrated his fire on this

24

battery exploding four of its caissons in quick succession. As the last section was retired a shot from his right piece exploded one of the Southern limbers.

When the firing ceased Capt. Cowan gave his attention to the casualties. Four of his enlisted men had been instantly killed, and one was mortally wounded; two officers, Lieutenants William P. Wright and William H. Johnson and six men were wounded, and Lt. Theodore Atkins was prostrated by sun-stroke. Lieutenant Peter Kelly having been left with the caissons, Andrew Cowan found himself the only officer on his feet at the end. He gathered up the remains of the young Confederate officer and buried them, together with the body of his friend, Capt. Rorty, in the soft soil of the depression in rear of the crest – the earth was too hard at the clump of trees.

The Twelfth Corps

The heavy timber and broken character of the ground on the right flank of Gen. Meade's defensive perimeter prevented the artillery brigade attached to the Twelfth Corps from taking position in the line proper to that Corps. It was therefore held in reserve and in readiness to answer all calls which might be made upon it. Three guns of Pennsylvania Independent Battery E, (Knap's), under Lt. Edward R. Geary, and one section of Lt. David H. Kinzie's (K, 5th US) led by Lt. William E. Van Reed, deployed on the crest of Culp's Hill and took an active part in the July 2 affair with Gen. Ewell's Second Corps artillery on Benner's Hill. Their fire was screened by the woods, but was so accurate and timely that it proved an important factor in the withdrawal of Ewell's Rebel guns. When the U.S. Twelfth Corps was ordered to the left, these guns were removed from Culp's Hill. Pennsylvania Battery E (Lt. Charles A. Atwell then in command), and Lt. Charles E. Winegar, (M, 1st NY) were sent to Powers' Hill, while Lt. Kinzie, (K, 5th US) and Lt. Sylvanus T. Rugg, (F, 4th US) remained in park at its base.

By 1:00 A.M. of July 3, Rugg and Kinzie were posted west of the Baltimore turnpike in rear of the center of the Twelfth Corps' tactical area, dominating the ravine formed by Rock Creek. Three and one-half hours later the four batteries (20 guns) opened and threw shot and shell for fifteen minutes into Gen. George H. Steuart's Confederates. These Rebels were then inside and in front of the Union entrenchments just below Culp's Hill which had been vacated the evening before. This artillery barrage began again at 5:30 A. M. and continued at intervals until

Gen. Edward Johnson's division gave up its hold on the Yankee entrenchments and retreated across Rock Creek. During this action Winegar's Battery was divided, the left section going to William McAllister's Hill east of the pike, the right section remaining to the west on Power's Hill. Due to an error in elevation, Rugg and Kinzie were exposed, in their sector along the Baltimore pike, to an incessant hail of projectiles from Alexander's Southern guns out at the Peach Orchard heights which were being directed toward Northern soldiers on Cemetery Ridge.

The Artillery Reserve

On the morning of the second day of the battle the reserve artillery, under the direction of Gen. Robert O. Tyler, was parked between the Baltimore turnpike and the Taneytown Road, south of the lane that passed the Granite schoolhouse. Tyler's men, if called upon, could continue along this narrow wagon path, which was simply an extension of the above lane, and enter the main Union battle line at about the center of the Third Corps' operational area. Going further to the west, his batteries would pass the George Weikert house, then after crossing Plum Run near the Catherine and Abraham Trostle buildings, would strike the Emmitsburg Road. About 3:00 P.M. Gen. Meade rode to the extreme left to await the arrival of the Fifth Corps, previously ordered to that point, and found, as he passed, Gen. Daniel Sickles in the earlier noted unsanctioned forward locality, with his corps already *un fait accompli*. Too late to rectify the error, Meade instructed Sickles that he would be supported from the Fifth Corps, and that he might also call for assistance from the Second Corps, and that he (Meade) would direct Gen. Hunt to send Sickles all the artillery he might ask for. This conference was broken by the artillery practice that preceded Longstreet's attack..

General Robert O. Tyler
Reserve Artillery Chief.

General Sickles' initial request

26

was upon the army's artillery reserve. Captain Nelson Ames, (G, 1st NY) was the first to respond and was posted by Capt. George E. Randolph, the artillery chief of the Third Corps, in Sherfy's peach orchard. Lieutenant Colonel McGilvery, who commanded a volunteer brigade of the reserve artillery was called upon next. It was fortunate that this excellent soldier had not been tempted, by the lure of promotion, from his arm of the service, for his country had great need of him that afternoon. McGilvery's Brigade was composed of four batteries: Capt. John Bigelow, (9th MA), Capt. Charles Phillips, (5th MA), Capt. Patrick Hart, (15th NY) and Capt. James Thompson, (C & F, 1st PA).

Bigelow and Phillips were aligned on the Millerstown Crossover Road (or Wheatfield Road) overlooking the open fields to the southwest and over toward John Rose's large stone house and barn. Thompson was posted in the Peach Orchard on the left of Ames, with Hart on his left; these batteries had a clear field of fire west and southwest.

General Winfield S. Hancock, to fill the gap between Sickles' right at the Peter Rogers house and the main Union line on Cemetery Ridge, in addition to two of Gen. William Harrow's regiments sent forward to the Nicholas Codori buildings, advanced Lt. Brown's (B, 1st RI) battery of his own corps to the rough ground in front of the Angle with the 72nd

Looking north from Ames' Battery, (G, 1ˢᵗ NY) at the Peach Orchard. The Spangler and Sherfy farm buildings are visible in the distance.

Pennsylvania in support. He also called up Capt. Dunbar R. Ransom's Brigade from the artillery reserve. This brigade was comprised of four regular army batteries: Lt. Chandler P. Eakin, (H, 1st US), Lt. John G. Turnbull, (F & K, 3rd US), Lt. Evan Thomas, (C, 4th US) and Lt. Gulian V. Weir, (C, 5th US). Captain Ransom came to the front with three of his batteries, dropping off Turnbull on the ridge near Gen. Meade's headquarters with Weir and Thomas in order named along the ridge to the south. Later, Ransom accompanied Turnbull's Battery to the Emmitsburg Road and placed it on the right of David Klingel's house in the spot just vacated by Lt. Francis W. Seeley, (K, 4th US), who was moved to the left, or south of the house. Ransom was severely wounded by a sharpshooter while putting this battery into line. Weir was moved forward some 500 yards from his first position, accompanied by one of Gen. Harrow's regiments, the 19th Maine. Lieutenant Thomas' pieces were directed to the front with Col. William Colvill's 1st Minnesota along to assist. Eakin's battery was sent to Evergreen Cemetery where he was subsequently wounded; the command then devolved upon Lt. Philip D. Mason. It therefore took seven batteries brought up from the artillery reserve to repair Sickles' error, besides breaking up Harrow's infantry brigade for the defense of the batteries on the right.

About 5:00 P. M. Gen. Joseph B. Kershaw's South Carolina brigade came forward to the attack. The right wing of Kershaw's Brigade was followed by Gen. Paul J. Semmes' troops against Col. P. Regis De Trobriand's Brigade in the south and southwest section of Rose's wheat field and on the high ground beyond. The left wing of Kershaw's force struck the south face of the salient at the Peach Orchard.   Ames', Thompson's and Hart's cannon concentrated their fire on single enemy batteries in their front, and on other Confederate artillery in the woods at canister range on their flank.   About 6:00 P.M. Barksdale's Mississippians, followed in support by Georgians under Gen. William T. Wofford, debouched from these woods less than 600 yards from the batteries emplaced in the Peach Orchard. Meanwhile Kershaw's Rebels had gained the woods west of the Wheatfield which exposed Bigelow's and Phillips' artillerymen to enemy sharpshooters. Somewhere close to 5:30 P.M. Capt. Ames, then out of ammunition, was replaced by Watson, a Fifth Corps "Regular's" battery taken by one of Sickles'aides from its position without the usual formalities. Half an hour later, the whole line of batteries was ordered by Lt. Col. McGilvery to retire to a new position 250 yards to the rear, and to renew their fire. Lieutenant Malbone Watson was wounded, and his battery drawn back under Lt. MacConnell, only to be overrun later by Barksdale's charging Southerners. Here, Capt. Hart's

New Yorkers, like Ames, were forced to leave the field with empty caissons. In Capt. Phillips' unit, Lt. Henry D. Scott and four men hauled off one of the pieces by hand, but abandoned a limber which was recovered on July 4. Lieutenant Scott was severely wounded in the face while bringing off this cannon. Captain Thompson had one of his rifled guns taken by the enemy in the Peach Orchard; it was engaged, at the moment of its capture facing west against Barksdale. Federal infantry rallied, and the gun was soon recaptured. The battery then limbered up and withdrew to its next fighting position, (about 300 yards to the east), where it once again went into action. When the infantry retreated, and the horses of a gun limber and a caisson limber were killed, Thompson's Pennsylvanians finally departed leaving one gun after hauling it a considerable distance by hand.

While Phillips and Thompson were still firing from this second stand, Capt. Bigelow retired from his first position, by prolonge, to an angle in a rock fence adjacent to the Trostle buildings.

Bigelow's initial combat had taken place along the Millerstown, or Wheatfield Road, east of the Peach Orchard. His left piece had rested on the road, and his field of fire saturated the ground over which Kershaw and later Semmes made their attacks. As this Massachusetts battery entered the battle zone through the gateway in the stone fence at the Trostle house, its members were greeted by a chorus of rapid and crashing volleys from the high ground to the west. These nerve-tightening sounds were emitted from the muskets of Gen. Charles K. Graham's Yankee regiments and the booming cannon of the Third Corps artillery. Three hours of the fiercest fighting at Gettysburg commenced as Bigelow's guns were whirled across the fields to the Wheatfield Road.

The sturdy oak cannon trails were soon dropped amid a heavy fire from sharpshooters and two Confederate batteries. Almost immediately one of Bigelow's men was killed and several others hit before they could let fly a single shot. During the action that followed, with Kershaw and Semmes pressing almost to the mouths of Bigelow's bronze cannon, this intrepid battery, in this their baptism of fire, began a service to the flag that ended at Appomattox twenty-one months later. While these tense and terrible moments played out, Gen. Andrew A. Humphrey's Division of the Third Corps, north of the orchard made a change of front, its left swinging back like a hinged gate, the right holding at the Rogers house on the Emmitsburg Road. General Charles K. Graham had been wounded and taken prisoner, and his brigade was fighting front and flank, and was forced back, with the artillery, through the fields across Bigelow's right. Meanwhile Barksdale regrouped his brigade at the Emmitsburg Road.

Once Barksdale had reformed his troops, he changed direction to meet Humphrey's new deployment, and plunged forward. Soon Wofford, in support, came crashing on, paralleling the Wheatfield Road. All of these unforgettable scenes passed by as Bigelow's battery was pulled off by prolonge, sending outward charges of deadly canister as it rolled back to the Trostle yard. Bigelow's 12-pounders were skillfully maneuvered to this point, his left section keeping Kershaw's skirmishers back with canister rounds while the other two sections engaged Barksdale's right which was pouring down the Trostle lane in quick time. But there was no rest yet, as Capt. Bigelow was soon halted by Col. McGilvery at the Trostle house, and ordered into an impossible position for artillery; Bigelow was instructed to hold at all cost until infantry could be found or batteries collected to fill the open gap between Little Round Top and the left of the Second Corps. The Massachusetts battery was now hemmed in by the angle of a rock fence, and one-half of its men and horses were already lying injured or dead. Regardless, Bigelow's gunners unlimbered, took the ammunition from the chests, and placed it near their pieces for rapid firing, then loaded the guns to the muzzle. As the murderous combat erupted, and just before the enemy closed in for the kill, Lt. Richard S. Milton succeeded in withdrawing the left section, one gun squeezed through the gateway in the wall, the other by making a gap in

Captain Bigelow's final position near the Trostle Farm

the rock fence. The remaining four guns continued to fire until they had to be abandoned as the Confederates swarmed in on their flanks, backed up by Alexander's guns at the Peach Orchard. In the thirty minutes between 6 and 6:30 Bigelow's battery finished its sacrifice. Lieutenant Christopher Erickson was shot through the lungs, but continued giving orders with a bloody froth dripping from his mouth, until he slid from his horse riddled with bullets. Captain Bigelow fell from his own horse, badly wounded, within 50 feet of the rock fence. Lieutenant Alexander H. Whittaker, though mortally wounded himself, rode up and gave Bigelow a drink from his flask. Captain Bigelow was then assisted onto the horse of his bugler Charles W. Reed and guided to safety by Reed directly through Lt. Edwin B. Dow's battery, (F, 6th ME) one of the units that had been gathered by McGilvery. For his calm bravery, Bugler Reed was awarded a Congressional Medal of Honor.

The "Plum Run Line" – July 2nd

Lieutenant Colonel McGilvery had succeeded in collecting a number of guns, (21 in all) east of Plum Run, 400 or 500 yards to the rear, covering the passage to the Taneytown Road. These cannon repelled several efforts to break through until, just after 7:00 P.M., Barksdale was driven back by Col. George L. Willard's Brigade, in which action both commanders were killed. One of Barksdale's regiments, the 21st Mississippi, after over-running Bigelow's guns, passed to the east of Plum Run where it took and held Watson's battery for a few minutes. This same battery was recaptured by the gallantry of Lt. Peeples as has been already told. Bigelow's casualties were high: two lieutenants killed, himself seriously wounded, and seven enlisted men killed and 16 wounded, with two missing. Six out of seven sergeants were dead or injured. Eighty out of 88 horses were killed and disabled. Of the 96 rounds of canister in the chests 92 rounds were used, making over three tons of ammunition expended in all.

The emergency line of guns gathered by McGilvery was composed of Watson, (I, 5th US), Dow, (F, 6th ME), part of Phillips, (5th MA) and part of Thompson, (C & F, 1st PA). During the entire afternoon Lt. Col. McGilvery escaped without injury despite fearlessly exposing himself to enemy missiles on all parts of the field from Cemetery Ridge to the Peach Orchard. His horse however was struck four times by bullets, once by a shell fragment, and again by a spent solid shot; death came soon after.

For a time too, the colonel also eluded recognition for services rendered, "on this fiery line."

The Emmitsburg Road

After Barksdale's attack, Gen. Cadmus M. Wilcox's Alabama and Col. David Lang's Florida brigades came forward, with Gen. Ambrose R. Wright's Georgians not far behind. Wilcox and Lang were slowed and held by Lt. Evan Thomas, (C, 4th US) and the 1st Minnesota until Col. William R. Brewster and Gen. Joseph B. Carr rallied their Third Corps brigades. These brigades reformed on Cemetery Ridge, and then charged the Confederates, driving them back to the Emmitsburg Road. General Harrow's two regiments, the 15th Massachusetts and 82nd New York, which were stationed north of the Codori buildings, were forced back by Wright's brigade, and each regiment lost its colonel. Wright's Georgians then overran Brown and Weir's batteries in advance of the main Union defensive line, and almost gained the wall at the Angle. They were finally checked near the crest of Cemetery Ridge among the Yankee guns by Col. Francis V. Randall with five companies of the 13th Vermont, who had come from the rear of Cemetery Hill followed by other regiments of Doubleday's division. Colonel Randall met Gen. Hancock who pointed out Wright's Rebel soldiers carrying off several cannons from Weir's battery. Randall followed them nearly to the Emmitsburg Road, recaptured the guns and brought them to safety. His Vermonters then returned to the vicinity of the Rogers house and took as prisoners three Southern officers and 80 men.

Captain John Turnbull, (F & K, 3rd US), had too been forced to retire, with a loss of Lt. Livingston and eight men killed and 14 wounded, in addition to the loss of 45 horses. Four guns of his battery were left near Klingel's house on the Emmitsburg Road; all were reclaimed by a counter-charge made by regiments of Brewster's brigade, who also brought off the flag of the 8th Florida along with 30 of its members.

Randolph's old Battery E, 1st Rhode Island, was the first in place facing west on the Emmitsburg Road north of the Peach Orchard. Lieutenant Bucklyn led this organization and was badly hurt when pried from his position by Barksdale's charge. Along the road, between Bucklyn and Turnbull, stood Lt. Francis Seeley's Battery (K, 4th US). At or about 5:30 P.M. Lt. Seeley was seriously injured, leaving Lt. Robert James to withdraw his Napoleons when all of their defending infantry had fallen back. As sunset approached, this battery was placed near Lt. Edwin B. Dow's (F, 6th ME) in McGilvery's evolving formation east of Plum

32

Run. When pushed from its station at the Klingel farm by Gen. Wilcox's Georgians, James wheeled his six Napoleons by the right and back some 400 yards to get a good fire on the Rebels' flank. The lieutenant had scarcely unlimbered when Lang's Florida Brigade skirmishers pushed right into Lt. James' artillerymen from its right flank. Besides Lt. Seeley, this close fight produced casualties of 23 wounded officers and men.

East Cemetery Hill

During that desperate afternoon Capt. James F. Huntington's volunteer brigade of the artillery reserve was ordered to report to Gen. Oliver O. Howard at Eleventh Corps' headquarters. Huntington soon had his units placed nearby. Lieutenant George W. Norton, (H, 1st OH), Capt. Frederick M. Edgell, (A, 1st NH), and Capt. Wallace Hill, (C, 1st WV) were located in Evergreen Cemetery facing north and west. Captain Elijah D. Taft's (5th NY) was also detailed to the cemetery, with four guns stationed along the Baltimore Pike side and two on the crest facing north toward town. Taft's was the only 20-pounder rifled battery with the Army of the Potomac at Gettysburg. The four guns along the turnpike were aimed eastward out to Benner's Hill, and played a roll in that affair, firing over the cannon of Lt. George Breck, then commanding Reynold's Battery (L, 1st NY) in lunettes on the lower ground in the front of Taft's 20-pounders. Breck later complained, and surely would have known, that some of their ammunition was defective. Captain Robert Bruce Rickett's (F & G, 1st PA) replaced Capt. James H. Cooper, (B, 1st PA) on East Cemetery Hill after the Benner's Hill duel.

Captain Ricketts' Pennsylvanians came to be known to the Confederates, on that night, as "Battery Hell." After his Second Corps artillery was driven from Benner's Hill late on July 2, Gen. Ewell began an evening attack on Culp's Hill with Johnson's Division. Ricketts, with neighboring units, opened fire on Gen. Edward Johnson's Rebels, the exploding projectiles following the Southerners into the woods west of Rock Creek, being guided along by the thick, grayish smoke of the infantry battle. Rickett's Battery was thus engaged when Col. Isaac E. Avery's and Gen. Harry T. Hays' Brigades developed their assault upon East Cemetery Hill from the eastern edge of the town. During this latter action there was a moment when Rickett alone contended with all of the men Hays and Avery had succeeded in getting to the crest of the hill, with the sole exception of some help delivered by the left section of Lt. Stewart, (B, 4th US) on the Baltimore Pike. Captain Ricketts stated that not an enemy soldier of these two brigades passed through the front of his battery; they came in on him from the rock fence on his left flank where they had been driven to shelter by Stewart's hurtling canister. From this fence they fired down the line of Rickett's guns; then with muskets against sponge-staffs, handspikes, and even stones, the Rebels fought the cannoneers back to their third piece. But in the end, there were not enough Confederates on the hill to force Rickett's veterans from their 3-inch rifles.

An important factor in this nighttime assault was the presence nearby of Steven's Battery E, 5th Maine. Just as the evening combat began, Capt. Stevens, finding ammunition running low, had the contents of his caissons transferred to the limbers, and then sent the caisson teams to the supply trains at Power's Hill to replenish. This left the battery with a scanty stock of shell, but plenty of case shot, and a bit of canister left over from the day before. The first order given as the Southerners came into view was for "case, two and one-half degrees, three seconds." The Maine gunners had a clear sweep across the northeast face of East Cemetery Hill. The Confederate regiments swerved to the right to escape this fire, which brought them under cover of the hill and the Pennsylvania cannon on its

Looking up Cemetery Hill toward the Evergreen Cemetery gatehouse and Union artillery pieces protected by earthworks.

On July 2 the 5ᵗʰ Maine Battery was stationed on a small knoll east of the Baltiimore Pike and south on East Cemetery Hill. During an evening attack on the latter hill by Confederate forces, Pvt. John F. Chase was loading a 12-pound case shot into one of the Napoleons. A premature discharge exploded the cannon ball, hitting Chase with 48 fragments and shrapnel balls. Left for dead, he was eventually carried to a field hospital where he slowly recovered. Despite losing an eye and one arm and suffering from over 40 wounds, John Chase lived a full life and died in 1914.

Captain Stevens' 5ᵗʰ Maine Artillery on McKnight's Hill

crest, with only Stevens' guns and Breck's right section available to thwart their movements. Stevens' men then served up the remaining canister, a hearty dish not at all appreciated by the Louisiana and North Carolina infantrymen who received it.

The "Plum Run Line" – July 3rd

Lieutenant Colonel Freeman McGilvery had done so well on the afternoon of the second day with his rag-tag collection of batteries placed on the low ground along Cemetery Ridge, that he was assigned to the same duty the following morning on the exact terrain. These instructions were in preparation for any attempt made to pierce the Federal center by Lee's Army of Northern Virginia. This July 3 deployment was composed of, Thomas, (C, 4th US), six guns; Thompson, (C & F, 1st PA), five guns; Phillips, (E, 5th MA), six guns; Hart, (15th NY), four guns; Capt. John W. Sterling, (2nd CT), four guns; Capt. William D. Rank, (H, 3rd PA), two guns; Dow, (F, 6th ME), four guns; and Ames, (G, 1st NY), six guns. These batteries were also added: Cooper, (B, 1st PA), four guns; Capt. Jabez J. Daniels, (9th MI), six guns; and Parsons, (A, 1st NJ), six guns. During the Confederate bombardment preceding Gen. Longstreet's attack,

a slow well-directed fire was concentrated on single Rebel batteries in McGilvery's front. This caused several of those units to be silenced, and driven successively to the rear. Subsequently, when the first Southern-assaulting lines appeared, they presented an oblique front to most of these Union batteries. After Pickett's Division had been broken and turned back, attention was given to Wilcox's Brigade which was stopped before he could come within the zone of most of the infantry musket-fire available in that sector.

Lt. Col. Freeman McGilvery

The Horse Artillery

The horse-artillery of the cavalry corps, Army of the Potomac, was composed of two brigades under Captains James M. Robertson, (M, 2nd

A portion of McGilvery's "Plum Run Line" along Cemetery Ridge.

US) and John C. Tidball, (A, 2nd US). Robertson detailed Lt. Alexander C.M. Pennington, (M, 2nd US), and Lt. Samuel S. Elder, (E, 4th US) to Gen. Judson Kilpatrick's division, and the two participated, with that division, in the cavalry skirmishes at Hanover and Hunterstown on June 30 and July 2, respectively. On the morning of July 3, Elder and Capt. William M. Graham, (K, 1st US) one of Tidball's batteries, accompanied Gen. Elon J, Farnsworth of the Third Division, Cavalry Corps, to the extreme left near Big Round Top. At the same time, Pennington, and Capt. Alanson M. Randol, (E & G, 1st US), also under Tidball, traveled with Gen. David M. Gregg's cavalry division to the Hanover Pike. Pennington and Randol were fortunate and had, on July 3 in the battle with Gen. James E.B. Stuart's Confederate horsemen, perhaps the best chance for artillery service during their military career. Success was not so prodigal with her favors to Elder and Graham on the left. Tidball's own battery under Lt. John H. Calef, (A, 2nd US) was the center of attention, as has been seen, on July 1, as it suffered, at 1300 yards, the concentrated fire of five, four-gun Southern batteries from Herr's Ridge. Battle experience was nothing new to Lt. Calef, but promotion lagged behind, as with other officers of the artillery corps. In fact, it was 12 years after Gettysburg before John Calef became a captain. He was breveted three times for gallant and meritorious conduct during his military career and finally retired with the grade of lieutenant colonel. Similarly, Lt. James Stewart, who had been a private, corporal, sergeant, first sergeant and lieutenant in the 4th United States Artillery, left the army in 1879 having only advanced, even with two brevets for gallant and meritorious service in the field, to the grade of captain. Regrettable stories like these were common, and clouded the otherwise excellent history of the field artillery in the army of the United States of America.

The country still remains in the debt of these dedicated artillerymen for the difficult services they rendered to the flag of the Union on the field of Gettysburg. The artillery brigades which fought on that deadly ground were composed of 217 officers and 7,329 men. Besides the grade of captain, only two officers of general rank and four of field rank commanded this sizable force. Memorializing the sacrifices of the artillery units at Gettysburg, in addition to cannon marking their battery positions, there was laid out in 1913 one avenue, and a single gun tube, without carriage, resting on its butt with muzzle pointing to the sky. As a comparison, the Twelfth Corps reported on June 30, 1863, 521 officers and 7,692 men present and equipped. It was officered by six generals and twenty-two officers of field rank. But in contrast, the fine battle history of that corps has been gloriously memorialized with an equestrian statue and four avenues bearing the names of four of its officers, along with many and various lesser monuments and markers. [10]

The Gettysburg National Military Park has on exhibit approximately 400 cannons marking the battery positions occupied by the two armies in 1863. While the gun carriages are all cast-iron reproductions, most of the barrels are original weapons. However, a number of the tubes are not real. Throughout the park visitors may notice that some of the iron cannon barrels are crude imitations. Serious casting flaws are apparent, and the military markings usually found on the muzzle, trunnion faces, and breech are missing.

This cannon is a reproduction with a seam visible along the length of the barrel.

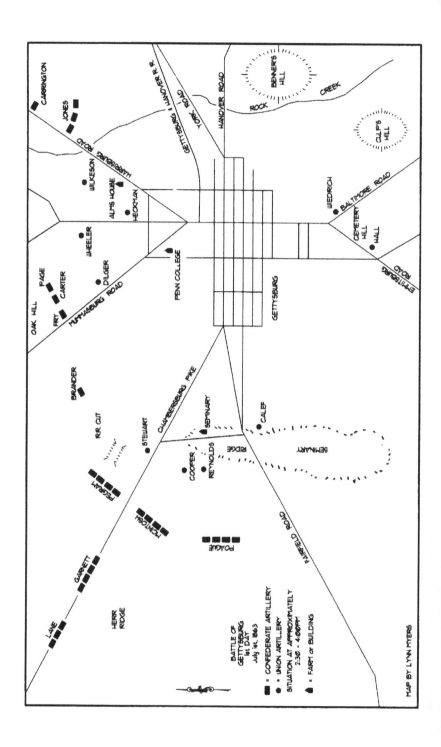

BATTLE OF
GETTYSBURG
1st DAY
July 1st, 1863

■ = CONFEDERATE ARTILLERY
● = UNION ARTILLERY
SITUATION AT APPROXIMATELY
2:30 - 4:00PM
▲ = FARM or BUILDING

MAP BY LYNN MYERS

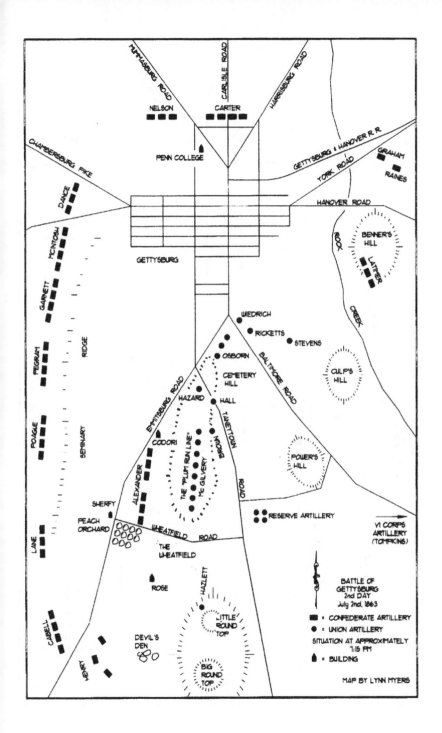

MUMMASBURG ROAD
CARLISLE ROAD
HARRISBURG ROAD

NELSON ▪▪▪
CARTER ▪▪▪▪

CHAMBERSBURG PIKE
PENN COLLEGE ▲

GETTYSBURG & HANOVER R.R.
YORK ROAD

GRAHAM ▪▪
RAINES

DANCE ▪▪

HANOVER ROAD

ROCK

BENNER'S HILL

McINTOSH ▪▪▪

GETTYSBURG

LATTIER ▪▪

CREEK

GARRETT ▪▪▪

RIDGE

WIEDRICH ●
RICKETTS ●
STEVENS ●

CULP'S HILL

PEGRAM ▪▪▪

OSBORN ●

EMMITSBURG ROAD

CEMETERY HILL

BALTIMORE ROAD

POAGUE ▪▪

SEMINARY

HAZARD ●
CODORI ●
THE "PLUM RUN LINE"
McGILVERY ●●

HALL ●

TANEYTOWN

BROWN

POWER'S HILL

SHERFY ●

ALEXANDER ▪▪

ROAD

RESERVE ARTILLERY ●●
●●

VI CORPS ARTILLERY (TOMPKINS) →

LANE ▪▪

PEACH ORCHARD ○○○○○
○○○

WHEATFIELD ROAD

THE WHEATFIELD

ROSE ▲

HAZLETT ▲

LITTLE ROUND TOP

BATTLE OF GETTYSBURG
2nd DAY
July 2nd, 1863

CABELL ▪▪

DEVIL'S DEN ○○○

BIG ROUND TOP

▪ = CONFEDERATE ARTILLERY
● = UNION ARTILLERY
SITUATION AT APPROXIMATELY 7:15 PM
▲ = BUILDING

HENRY ▪▪

MAP BY LYNN MYERS

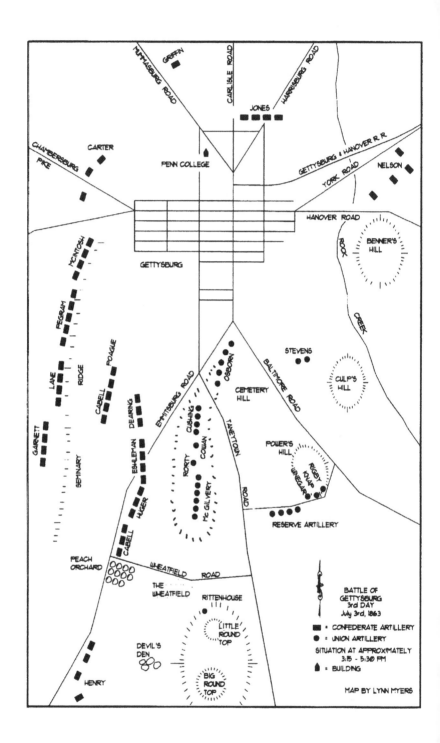

The Army of Northern Virginia

The artillery of the armies of the Confederate States of America was generally outclassed throughout the four years of the American Civil War except in organization and fighting spirit. At the beginning of the year 1863, Gen. Robert E. Lee, the commander of the Army of Northern Virginia was not satisfied that the existing policy of attaching batteries to brigades and grouping them in divisions was promoting the best results in that arm of the service. His chief of artillery, Gen. William N. Pendleton, was directed to formulate a plan for a better organization of the artillery. The objections to brigade batteries and division groups were obvious; it was impossible for brigade and division commanders to find time, burdened by the duties of their large infantry units, to devote proper supervision of the batteries assigned to them; nor did the arrangement afford any wider scope of authority for the field officers of the artillery.

In consultation with Colonels Stapleton Crutchfield and Edward P. Alexander, Gen. Pendleton drew up a design for the reorganization which then was forwarded to Gen. Lee. This proposal, with some modifications, was accepted and made effective under Special Order No. 106, April 16th, 1863. The batteries were arranged into battalions, each battalion to

General William N. Pendleton.

consist of four, four-gun batteries with two field officers to every sixteen guns. It was recommended that batteries should be rendered homogeneous in armament as soon as practicable by the interchange of cannon tubes with other units. This rendered the army fifty-nine batteries, thirty-five from Virginia, and twenty-four from the other states. Twenty-eight field officers were authorized, care being taken to observe the same proportion of field officers to batteries between Virginia and the other Southern states. Of the twenty-eight field officers accepted, eighteen were Virginians.

Twenty-six batteries (112 guns) were assigned under this reorganization to Gen. James Longstreet's First Corps, making six battalions with twelve field officers. Twenty-seven batteries containing 116 guns, in six battalions, with twelve field officers were allotted to Gen. Thomas J. Jackson's Second Corps. Two battalions of three batteries each, (36 guns) constituted a general reserve with four officers of field rank. Of the above six battalions for the two corps, two battalions were withheld as a corps reserve. The ranking field officer in each corps was designated as the artillery chief for his corps.

After the Battle of Chancellorsville and Gen. Jackson's death, a new organization of the Army of Northern Virginia was designed that added a third infantry corps. This change induced a readjustment of Lee's artillery arm. Five battalions were assigned to each corps. Three of the battalions were employed as corps artillery, while two battalions were still slotted as a corps reserve. Under this refinement, the general reserve was broken up and its batteries distributed. General Pendleton was retained as chief of artillery. The fine hand of Col. Alexander is observed in this final updated recast, and served as a model for the armies of Europe after the Civil War.

During the Battle of Gettysburg, the artillery of Longstreet's Corps consisted of five battalions under Col. Henry C. Cabell, Maj. James Dearing, Maj. Mathias W. Henry, Col. Edward P. Alexander, and Maj. Benjamin F. Eshleman. Altogether Longstreet had twenty-one batteries and eighty-four guns, with Col. James B. Walton as head of the reserve and chief artillery officer of the corps. General Richard S. Ewell's Second Corps artillery comprised the battalions of Col. Hilary P. Jones, Maj. Joseph W. Latimer, Lt. Col. Thomas H. Carter, Capt. Willis J. Dance and Lt. Col. William Nelson. This provided a combination of twenty-one batteries and eighty-four guns, with Col. J. Thompson Brown as head of the reserve and chief artillery officer of the corps. General Ambrose P. Hill's Third Corps artillery was made up of the battalions of Maj. John Lane, Lt. Col. John J. Garnett, Maj. William T. Poague, Maj. David G. McIntosh and Maj. William J. Pegram. This configuration allotted a total of twenty batteries and eighty guns. The head of the reserve and the corps chief of artillery was Col. R. Lindsay Walker. The six batteries assigned to Gen. James E. B. Stuart's cavalry division were led by Maj. Robert F. Beckham, who succeeded Stuart's lamented friend, Maj. John Pelham, killed at Kelly's Ford, VA, March 16, 1863.

Since the Army of Northern Virginia became offensive in tactics as well as in strategy in the Pennsylvania Campaign, the Confederate artillery did not have the same opportunities to shine as those afforded the

Federal batteries. In Lee's army, there would be few if any headlines written for cannons fighting skirmish lines with canister, or gray-clad gunners meeting bayonets with hand-spikes and sponge staffs.

The battles at Gettysburg began, as the unexpected always does, before the Southern forces were completely prepared for a confrontation. The Third Corps under Gen. Hill was the first to become engaged, followed by Gen. Ewell's Second Corps, and finally the First Corps led by Gen. Longstreet. General Hill was always ready for a fight, and had on occasion precipitated a battle when he should have been restrained by his superiors. He allowed the trouble at Gettysburg to begin without the knowledge of or orders from his commanding general. If it had not been for the fortuitous arrival of the divisions of Generals Robert E. Rodes and Jubal A. Early on the weak flank of his enemy, he may have been disastrously defeated along Edward McPherson's ridge on July 1. General Oliver O. Howard's seizure of Oak Ridge could have turned his position on Herr's Ridge, compelling him to fall back on his supports at Cashtown.

Hill's Third Corps

At the beginning of the campaign in Pennsylvania Lt. Col. Garnett's Battalion was ordered to report for duty to the division of Gen. Henry Heth; Maj. Poague's Battalion was sent to the division of Gen. William D. Pender; and Maj. Lane's Battalion was placed with Gen. Richard H. Anderson's Division. The battalions of Majors McIntosh and Pegram constituted Hill's Corps reserve. This corps arrived at Fayetteville, PA on June 27, and remained there two days. The recent marches on the hard-surfaced Shenandoah Valley turnpike of Virginia had been grueling on the horses' feet; therefore, from the Fayetteville encampment a foraging party was sent out to procure fresh animals. This party made some seizures, but encountered a detachment of Yankee cavalry which recaptured the horses, together with Lt. John H. Chamberlayne and four men of Lt. Andrew Johnston's [W.G. Crenshaw's] (VA) Battery of Pegram's Battalion. On June 30, McIntosh's, Pegram's and Garnetts' battalions were in the vicinity of Cashtown, PA, with Lane and Poague's battalions under marching orders for that same village. Colonel R. Lindsay Walker arrived at Cashtown on this date and assumed command of all of the artillery of the Third Corps.

General Heth's Division broke camp at 5:00 A.M. on July 1, and was soon stretched out, with Pegram's batteries interspersed in the column, on their way eastward to Gettysburg. The units forming Maj. Pegram's battalion were Lt. Johnston's (VA), Capt. Edward A. Marye's (VA), Capt. Thomas A. Brander's (VA), Capt. William E. Zimmerman's (SC), and Capt. Joseph McGraw's (VA), five, four-gun batteries. Arriving within two miles of Gettysburg, a section of Marye's battery was unlimbered on the Chambersburg pike near the Belmont school house and opened fire on John Herbst's woodlot, also incorrectly known as McPherson's Grove. After letting eight or ten rounds fly, the section mounted up and, with the rest of battalion, deployed on Herr's Ridge. During the engagement that followed, the battalion used seventeen guns; its two 12-pounder howitzers were not put into action, and one of Capt. Zimmerman's rifled pieces was disabled going into the fight.

The battalion took an active part in the battles of the second and third days from Seminary Ridge nearly opposite the center of the Union lines. The casualties for the three days' engagement were 10 dead, 37 wounded and 1 missing; the ordnance officer, Lt. John Morris, Jr. was slain on the morning of July 1. The ammunition expended was 3,800 rounds. The battalion had 89 horses killed, 11 captured and 50 abandoned, plus two guns disabled, one caisson lost and four damaged.

Major David McIntosh's Battalion was composed of the batteries of Capt. R. Sidney Rice, (VA), Capt. William B. Hurt, (AL), Lt. Samuel Wallace, (VA), and Capt. Marmaduke Johnson, (VA). It moved with Pender's Division on the morning of July 1, and was present that day in the army's order of battle. Rice, Hurt (with a section of British Whitworth rifles), and Wallace were engaged on Herr's Ridge near the Cashtown or Chambersburg Pike, Johnson, and Hurt's remaining section, went out the Herr's Ridge Road to the "old mill road" where they went

By 1863, the Confederate Arsenal in Augusta GA could produce one 12-pounder Napoleon every two days. This same facility could also produce 7,000 pound of black powder at a cost of four cents per pound.

into battery, but remained inactive during the day. The Confederate artillery units on Herr's Ridge were employed to good advantage enfilading the railroad cut, Union Gen. Lysander Cutler's left wing, and later Col. Roy Stone's men in their change of front to the right. On July 2, the battalion was posted in Elizabeth Shultz's woods immediately south of the Fairfield Road. Here, in an interchange of missiles with the Federal batteries on Cemetery Hill, Lieutenants J.W. Tullis and G.A. Ferrell of Hurt's Battery were wounded. During the morning of the third day the two Whitworth guns were moved to Oak Hill where they remained until Lee's retreat late on July 4. One of these breech-loaders was damaged by a Union projectile on July 1, and it was again put out of commission by its own recoil two days later. McIntosh's casualties in men, killed and wounded were 24; in men captured, 16. Losses in animals; killed, 35; captured, 13; and 20 were abandoned. Ammunition expended was 1,249 rounds, mostly shell, and the battalion recorded the additional destruction of two caissons.

At 11:00 A.M. on July 1, Lt. Col. John Garnett's Battalion, at Cashtown was ordered to move towards Gettysburg. The battalion was halted in column on the side of the pike west of Herr's Ridge in the order named: Capt. Victor Maurin, (LA), Capt. Joseph D. Moore, (VA), Capt. John W. Lewis, (VA), and Capt. Charles R. Grandy, (VA). With the exception of Maurin's Battery, which was sent to relieve one of Maj. Pegram's batteries which was out of ammunition, the battalion was not engaged. On the morning of Thursday, July 2, the nine rifled pieces of this battalion under Maj. Charles Richardson were sent to Seminary Ridge where they were engaged all day. On the third day, these pieces were ordered to the right in support of Gen. Richard H. Anderson's Division where they were soon joined by the remaining guns of the battalion, and placed in rear of the ridge south of David McMillan's woods. Two rifled cannon belonging to Capt. Lewis' (VA) Battery of this battalion were subsequently abandoned, and captured by the Federals on the night of the retreat from Maryland. The loss in men was five wounded and 17 captured. Thirteen horses were killed, 26 captured, and 40 abandoned, with two guns and six caissons lost. About 1,000 rounds of ammunition was expended in all.

Major William Poague's Battalion took no part in the battles of the first and second days. Late in the evening of July 2, he reported for service to Gen. Richard H. Anderson, where 10 of his pieces were positioned on Seminary Ridge. The remaining guns, (six howitzers) were held a short distance behind the ridge. Of the 10 guns left on station, three rifles and two smoothbore Napoleons were aligned on the left of

Anderson's infantry and on the right of Maj. Pegram's guns. These five guns belonged to Capt. James W. Wyatt, (VA), and Capt. Joseph Graham, (NC), and were overseen by Capt. Wyatt. Five 12-pounders belonging to the batteries of Capt. George Ward, (MS), and Capt. James V. Brooke, (VA), were sent forward toward the Emmitsburg Road. There these weapons occupied ground in front of Gen. Ambrose R. Wright's Brigade of Richard Anderson's Division. These five guns were under the direction of Capt. Ward and they remained here during the cannonade that preceded Longstreet's assault on the afternoon of July 3.

Early in the forenoon of the third day, by order of Gen. Ambrose P. Hill, the five guns under Wyatt, (sitting about 400 yards north of Henry Spangler's woods) opened on Cemetery Ridge, and were immediately replied to by Yankee artillery. It was not then known to the Southerners, but they had sighted onto the exact range of Gen. George Meade's army headquarters at the Lydia Leister farmhouse behind that ridge. As Capt. Wyatt did not know the origin of the order for opening this bombardment, he ceased offensive actions after losing eight of his best horses. The six howitzers of Maj. William Poague's Battalion were then brought up to the main line and placed in protective lunettes on Seminary Ridge. Later on, in the waning afternoon hours of July 3, the broken fragments of Gen. George E. Pickett's brigades attempted unsuccessfully to rally behind these earthworks.

Major John Lanes' "Sumter Battalion" came to the field with Gen. Richard Anderson's Division, and bivouacked during the night of July 1 among his infantrymen. Captain Hugh M. Ross' (GA) Battery accompanied Gen. Cadmus M. Wilcox's Brigade on the Fairfield Road, out toward Black Horse Tavern, for picket duty. On the morning of the second day, when Anderson's Division began a march to its assigned location on Seminary Ridge, Capt. George M. Patterson's (GA) Battery of two Napoleons and four howitzers, plus one howitzer of Ross' Battery, reported to Wilcox, the leading brigade, and took position, after their formation was established on the higher ground south of Spangler's Woods. Captain John T. Wingfield, (GA), with two 20-pounder Parrotts and three 3-inch navy Parrotts, and the remaining guns of Hugh Ross' Battery, (three 10-pounders, and one 3-inch navy Parrott), went to the left of Anderson's Division north of Henry Spangler's woodlot. Here, these two batteries participated in the heavy work of both the second and third day's combat. Captain Patterson was only engaged during July 2 with Union batteries along the Emmitsburg Road, and came away with two killed and five injured, in addition to seven horses destroyed or disabled. Wingfield and Ross suffered the death of one artilleryman, with 14 wounded, plus 29 horses.

Ewell's Second Corps

The artillery assigned to Gen. Richard S. Ewell's Second Corps was directed by Col. J. Thompson Brown and was composed of the battalions of Col. Hilary Jones, Maj. Joseph Latimer, Lt. Col. Thomas Carter, Capt. Willis Dance and Lt. Col. William Nelson. Lieutenant Colonel Carter's Battalion came to the field with Gen. Robert E. Rodes' Division, and was the first into battle when Rodes deployed astride Oak Ridge. The artillery units of Capt. William P. Carter, (VA), and Capt. Charles W. Fry, (VA), went up to Oak Hill, and from there fired into the flank of Northern troops engaged with Gen. A. P. Hill's Third Corps. This cannonade was responded to by Capt. James H. Cooper's Battery B, 1st Pennsylvania, and Capt. Gilbert H. Reynolds, (L & E, 1st NY), with a steady accuracy which killed four men of Capt. Carter's Battery outright and wounded seven.

When, on that afternoon, Gen. George Doles' Brigade of Rodes' Division advanced toward Gettysburg across the open plain on the east side of the ridge, Gen. Rodes directed two batteries to follow in support, Capt. Richard C.M. Page, (VA), and Capt. William J. Reese, (AL), who were posted at the foot of the ridge on the east side, south of the Moses McClean farmhouse. Captain Hubert Dilger, (I, 1st OH), and Lt. William Wheeler, (13th NY), who with their units were in clear view of these Confederates near the Carlisle Road, shot into them with what proved to be a very destructive counter-fire. Captain Page's men especially suffered, with four men killed and mortally wounded, and 26 others more or less severely injured, and 17 horses killed and disabled. It was feared that Doles' Brigade would be forced back by the enemy in his front and on his left, thus exposing the flank of the division; consequently, Capt. Carter's Virginia Battery was brought over from the other side of the ridge and joined Reese and Page at the foot of the heights in Doles' rear. With the arrival of Gen. Jubal Early's Division, the whole Federal Eleventh Corps was driven back on the town. Southern batteries on the east side of the ridge pursued the fleeing Yankees, unlimbering a few pieces from time to time to break up the troops who rallied behind the small hillocks and swales. Lieutenant Colonel Carter's Battalion was not engaged during the second day. On July 3, 10 of his rifled cannon were in use on Seminary Ridge north and south of the railroad cut. The projectiles from these guns

A Confederate Napoleon of Page's Battery on Oak Hill is aimed at Dilger's Ohio guns in the fields below.

were directed into the Union batteries on Cemetery Hill to divert their fire from Pickett's and Pettigrew's foot soldiers in their charge across the fields in front of the Angle on Cemetery Ridge. The smoothbore Napoleons of the battalion were held in readiness in rear of Pennsylvania College, north of Gettysburg, but were not called into service.

The battalion of Lt. Col. Hilary Jones, marching with Gen. Early's Division and made up of the batteries of Capt. James M. Carrington, (VA), Capt. William A. Tanner, (VA), Capt. Charles A. Green, (LA), and Capt. Asher W. Garber, (VA), arrived with the division by the Heidlersburg Road to find Gen. Rodes' infantry units murderously engaged with the Federal First Corps, and his left brigade in serious trouble against Gen. Carl Schurz' Division of the Eleventh Corps. Jones' artillery pieces were at once driven over to high ground east of the Harrisburg Road overlooking Rock Creek, and commenced an attack on Lt. Wilkeson's Yankee gunners, (G, 4th US) on David Blocher's hill, (Barlow Knoll) and the Union infantry confronting Doles.

When Gen. John B. Gordon's Brigade advanced to the support of Doles, this fire was soon blanketed by Gordon's lines and had to be discontinued. It was again resumed farther to the left as the Yankee forces were withdrawn to the town. General Early instructed Capt. Carrington to cross Rock Creek in pursuit, but before he could comply, Gen. Harry T. Hays' Louisianians were in his way pushing the enemy into Gettysburg. While firing from their first position, three guns were disabled by having shot wedged in the bores and one gun was permanently ruined by a solid shot, probably sent from Dilger's Ohio Battery, that struck it squarely on the muzzle. This Napoleon 12-pounder was replaced by the gun taken from Capt. Lewis Heckman, (K, 1st OH), by Hays' Brigade. Just before sunset on July 2, Capt. Green was detached, with his Parrott rifle section, to Gen. Wade Hampton at Hunterstown, and remained with that cavalry command until the end of the third day. Captain Tanner's unit went to Gen. William Smith's Brigade on the afternoon of July 2, and coordinated with that brigade on the York Pike until the following morning. With the exceptions before noted, this battalion was not engaged in the battles of the second and third days.

Lieutenant Colonel R. Snowden Andrew's Battalion of artillery, assigned to Gen. Edward Johnson's Division of Ewell's Corps, was commanded during most of the campaign by Maj. Joseph W. Latimer, as Snowden was severely wounded before crossing the Potomac.

The battalion marched with Johnson's Division from Carlisle by way of Shippensburg, Scotland, Fayetteville and Cashtown, arriving at Gettysburg on the evening of July 1 just before dark. After nightfall, Maj. Latimer moved the battalion to the east of Gettysburg, and went into bivouac. At dawn, he examined the ground in his front and selected Christian Benner's hill for his batteries. About 4:00 P.M., Maj. Latimer was directed by Gen. Johnson, through the corps artillery chief, to assume the offensive. Fourteen guns were then run onto the hill. They were led by Capt. William D. Brown, (MD), who went to the right near the Hanover pike, Capt. John C. Carpenter, (VA), poised in the center, with Capt. William F. Dement, (MD), and one section of Capt. Charles I. Raine, (VA), on the left at the crown of the hill. The remaining section, (two 20-pounder Parrotts) was placed with Capt. Archibald Graham's (VA) Battery of Capt. Willis J. Dance's Battalion, in the rear of the right of the line.

Between 4 and 5:00 P.M. all twenty cannon, (six of them 20-pounders) engaged U.S. batteries on East Cemetery Hill. The fire was answered by First and Eleventh Corps units and Capt. Taft's (NY) Battery from Evergreen Cemetery, East Cemetery Hill and James McKnight's hill, the present day Stevens' Knoll. Pennsylvania Battery E, and a section of Lt. David Kinzie's (K, 5th US), were stationed on Culp's Hill, from whence they served an enfilading fire against the crowded

A Napoleon of Dement's Battery. Confederate guns here on Benner's Hill suffered heavily from Union artillery fire from Culp's Hill, McKnight's Hill, and Cemetery Hill.

Confederates on Benner's Hill, causing heavy casualties to Carpenter's Battery in the center. The Federal artillery was well served, and poured in a destructive bombardment which rendered the hill untenable. Major Latimer sent his sergeant-major to Gen. Johnson to say that he was unable to hold the heights any longer. Johnson told him to withdraw it if he deemed it prudent. In the contest, Capt. Brown was shot down, a gun was disabled, and his detachment so reduced that he could work but one section. Captain Dement had one caisson exploded, and the others emptied. These factors led Latimer to retire his broken force, leaving only four cannon on the crest to repel any possible advance of Northern infantry.

Soon after when Johnson's Division began its late evening attack on Culp's Hill, the young major attempted to cover the troops with the two pair of guns left on the hill. This drew upon him a terribly accurate counter-fire from the Yankee gunners on East Cemetery Hill, which soon caused his death. The command of the battalion immediately devolved upon Capt. Raine, who fell back a safe distance and encamped for the night. On the morning of July 3, Raine parked the battalion near the ordnance trains, refilled his empty caissons, and returned that evening to the front. The battalion then retired with the division during the evening to Oak Ridge. The casualties were besides Maj. Latimer, Capt. Brown and

A 10-pounder Parrott projectile, using a standard load of one pound, could at 400 yards, penetrate nearly six feet of wood. And a 12-pounder Napoleon projectile fired at 1,000 yards with a two-and-one-half pound charge, could penetrate 11-1/2 inches of oak.

Lt. William Roberts badly injured, in addition to 10 men killed, 32 wounded, and 80 horses left dead on the field. To this sum, Carpenter's Battery, which unfortunately held the center, contributed five soldiers to the death list and 19 seriously wounded, more than half the loss sustained by the battalion. Carpenter's unit was battered mostly from Culp's Hill, as the Union pieces there had their exact range.

The artillery reserve of Ewell's Second Corps was made up of the battalions of Capt. Willis Dance and Lt. Col. William Nelson. Their batteries came upon the scene on the evening of Wednesday, July 1, too late to take part in the work of the day. Captain Archibald Graham's (VA) Battery, (from Dance), as noted, was delegated to Lt. Col. Hilary P. Jones for service on the extreme left, and was active in the affair at Benner's Hill. The other four batteries of Dance's Battalion rested for the night, and early on July 2, Lt. John M. Cunningham, (VA), Captains David Watson, (VA), and Benjamin H. Smith, Jr., (VA), under the leadership of Lt. Col. Carter, were moved into service, while Lt. Charles B. Griffin's [Hupp's] "Salem Artillery" of Virginia was held in reserve in rear of the Seminary. Watson was posted on the ridge south of the railroad cut, Smith on his right near the Seminary, and Cunningham on the left of the Fairfield Road. At approximately 4:00 P.M. these three batteries commenced a cannonade, which continued until dark, most of it directed toward, and guided by the gunsmoke of the Yankee artillery on East Cemetery Hill, which was then engaged with Latimer on Benner's Hill. On July 3, Watson and Smith were shifted to the right (or south) of the Fairfield Road, along with two rifled guns belonging to Lt. Griffin's Battery. From there these cannon dueled with Federal artillery on Cemetery Hill and Cemetery Ridge until the end of Gen. James Longstreet's assault. That night all of the batteries were sent to the rear, leaving Griffin's two Napoleons on the ridge north of the railroad cut, where they remained throughout July 4. In the evening hours, Dance's Battalion followed Johnson's Division in retreat along the Fairfield Road. Captain Graham's Battery rejoined them very late on the third day. The total unit loss was three enlisted men killed and Lt. William M. Brown and 18 others wounded. The injured and sick of the battalion were captured by Union cavalry on the retreat to Williamsport.

After the battalion of Lt. Col. William Nelson joined Gen. Robert Rodes, Nelson was sent to report to Lt. Col. Carter. Early on July 2, Carter instructed Lt. Col. Nelson to place three batteries in rear of Oak Ridge overlooking the town. At 11:00 A.M. his batteries moved southward to Pennsylvania College to await events. All was quiet in that sector, so at dark, his units returned to the ridge. At dawn on July 3, Nelson was directed to join Gen. Johnson's Division on the left of Ewell's Corps. After this transition was completed, Lt. Col. Nelson parked his guns under the screen of Benner's Hill until midday, when he advanced to the ground held by Capt. Archibald Graham, and with that battery bombarded the Union Cemetery Hill artillery positions with the intent to divert their attention from Longstreet's and Hill's infantry assault that afternoon. Fortunately for the Yankee infantry posted near Evergreen Cemetery, this shooting only involved 20 or 25 rounds, and why it was discontinued is unknown. But it was very destructive while it lasted. General Oliver O. Howard recorded that in one of his Eleventh Corps regiments, "twenty-seven [men] fell at a single shot." At midnight on July 3, the battalion returned to its former bivouac of the previous day, where, supported by a brigade from Johnson's Division, it remained until Lee retreated from Pennsylvania. This battalion was a small one with only three batteries attached, those of Capt. Thomas J. Kirkpatrick, (VA), Capt. John L. Massie, (VA), and Capt. John Milledge, (GA).

Longstreet's First Corps

Gen. James Longstreet's First Corps artillery was called upon for more arduous service than fell to the lot of the other battalions in the Army of Northern Virginia. Three of his battalions, those of Maj. Mathias W. Henry, (Gen. John B. Hood's Division), Maj. Henry C. Cabell, (Gen. Lafayette McLaws' Division), and Col. Edward P. Alexander, (corps reserve), arrived at 9:00 A.M. on July 2, and eventually participated in Longstreet's battle on the U.S. left flank.

Early on the morning of the second day, Gen. William N. Pendleton, the artillery chief of Lee's army, with Colonels Armistead L. Long, and R. Lindsay Walker, and Capt. Samuel R. Johnston, made a careful survey of the Union positions. This reconnaissance was made from the extreme right of the Confederate line as then established on Seminary Ridge. Its purpose was to form an estimate of the ground, and to ascertain, if possible, the chances of success for an attack on the Union left, should the Round Tops offer no insuperable obstacle. Returning from this scout, the officers passed by the right and rear along a ravine road that skirted Willoughby's Run to the Fairfield Road. General Pendleton recorded, that, "...from an elevated point I could see the Federal cavalry and bodies of infantry and artillery moving along the Emmitsburg Road to their main line." He also revealed, it was "...about mid-day [when] Gen. Longstreet arrived and viewed the ground." One of Longstreet's first actions was to ask Col. Alexander to attempt to get a good view of the front, so shortly thereafter Pendleton conducted Alexander to the advanced point of observation previously visited. This examination was conducted after the arrival of the U.S. Third Corps brigades of Colonels George C. Burling and P. Regis De Trobriand by the Emmitsburg Road, and was rendered somewhat hazardous by the strong presence of Yankee marksmen. A noontime skirmish between Gen. Cadmus Wilcox's Alabama regiments, and Col. Hiram Berdan's U.S. sharpshooters and its supporting infantry (3rd ME) had cleared Samuel Pitzer's woodlot, so it seemed practicable that the terrain farther to the south could be visited. General Pendleton explained: "I therefore rode in that direction, and, when about to enter the woods met the commanding general, en route himself for a survey of the ground." As the engagement in Pitzer's woods ended about 1:00 P.M., Gen. Lee was likely in this location shortly after that hour. Pendleton then, in the company of Gen. Wilcox, continued his sightings southward, reaching as far as the James Warfield house and blacksmith shop. After noting the terrain features, enemy batteries and troops, etc., he returned to Gen. Longstreet to conduct his column to Warfield's, and supervise, if necessary, the disposition of his artillery. Meanwhile Lafayette McLaw's Division of Longstreet's Corps had been marched and counter-marched in and along the Marsh Creek Valley, guided by an officer of Gen. Lee's staff, to locate a secure, screened route to an area along Seminary Ridge, east of Pitzer's school, from which the day's surprise attack could be spearheaded. Longstreet, knowing that Gen. Lee expected an attack to soon begin, and impatient at the delay, finally instructed Gen. Hood, whose division had not been a part of McLaw's exploration of the Marsh Creek Valley, to push forward by the most direct route to the point designated for the attack. At some juncture on the march he met Pendleton, took his statement, and sent him on to hasten up the artillery. Cabell's, Alexander's and Henry's battalions soon arrived and the whole column started toward their tactical placements. Colonel Edward Alexander, to whom the field work for the day had been allotted, looked at the ground farther to the right, then put Henry's Battalion, with Maj. John C. Haskell sharing command responsibility, adjacent to Hood's Division on the ridge east of the Emmitsburg Road, and south of Joseph

54

Sherfy's peach orchard. Colonel Henry Cabell's Battalion traveled up the road from the Pitzer schoolhouse to the crest of Seminary Ridge, turned to the south and unlimbered along the ridge with the right guns resting on the Emmitsburg Road. His batteries were posted as follows: Capt. John C. Fraser, (GA), Capt. Edward S. McCarthy, (VA), Capt. Basil C. Manly, (NC), and Capt. Henry H. Carlton, (GA), from right to left in the order named. For the upcoming work, Alexander also delegated three of the batteries from his own battalion, under Maj. Frank Huger. They were Capt. George V. Moody, (LA), Capt. William W. Parker, (VA), and Lt. S. Capers Gilbert, [Rhett's] (SC), and all were aligned to the left of Cabell's Battalion, which lengthened the file of cannon to the old Millerstown crossover road, now called the "Wheatfield" Road.

At about 3:45 P.M., Alexander initiated the battle with the booming sound of 36 guns, 18 of Cabell's Battalion screening the troops of Gen. Joseph B. Kershaw, and 18 of his own battalion protecting the brigade of Gen. William Barksdale. They all were aimed at Union Third Corps units in and near the Peach Orchard and along the Emmitsburg Road, at ranges generally between 500 and 700 yards. Alexander held back eight of his own guns and ten of Maj. Benjamin F. Eshleman's Battalion in reserve.

The battalion assigned to Gen. John Hood's Division was that of Maj. Mathias W. Henry, and was composed of Capt. Alexander C. Latham, (NC), Capt. Hugh R. Garden, (SC), Capt. William K. Bachman, (SC), and Capt. James Reilly's (NC) batteries. Latham and Garden were set to work in front, to cover the advance of the left wing of the division, while Bachman and Reilly covered the movement of the right wing. Latham and Garden were engaged at from 1,100 to 1,400 yards. Their rifled pieces were effective against the Peach Orchard and nearby targets at the latter distance, and also with the guns of Federal Captains James E. Smith, (4th NY), and George B. Winslow, (D, 1st NY), on their left front at 1,000 and 1,200 yards. Bachman and Reilly also traded shots with Smith's Battery at Devil's Den, and during that encounter one of Reilly's 3-inch rifles burst. The three 10-pounder Parrotts later captured at Devil's Den from Capt. Smith by Southern infantrymen, replaced Reilly's disabled piece, plus a six-pounder and a 12-pounder howitzer; the carriages of the latter two cannon were abandoned on the retreat.

With Henry's Battalion in action, Col. Henry Cabell began his attack at about 700 yards from Sherfy's peach orchard. The clear terrain near Cabell's units gave little protection from enemy ordnance, which resulted in rapid destruction of both men and horses. Eighteen guns of Alexander's Battalion, under Maj. Huger, were put in on Cabell's left at canister range to the Yankee batteries at the Peach Orchard. This made a total of fifty-four Confederate cannon giving protective coverage before and during Longstreet's fight. However, precise counter-battery fire from the Northern Peach Orchard batteries dismounted two Southern guns, and caused such persistent injury to his cannoneers that Alexander was compelled to ask Barksdale for men to help handle the heavy 24-pounder howitzers belonging to Capt. Moody's Battery. It also forced a call-up of Captains Pichegru Woolfolk, Jr., (VA), and Tyler Jordan, (VA), the two batteries that had been left in reserve. As these two last-named units galloped up, Barksdale's Mississippians, followed by Woolfolk, swept through the Confederate guns, and charged the Union defenders. This impetuous attack broke the Peach Orchard salient, and drove back both the Federal artillery and Gen. Charles Graham's Brigade from the heights along the Emmitsburg Road. It also compelled the second division of Gen. Andrew A. Humphrey's U.S. Third Corps, farther up the road, to change its battle front from west to south to meet the onslaught. In an unusual but effective maneuver, the six batteries of Alexander's Battalion, (under Maj. Huger), quickly mounted and limbered their complement of personnel, weapons and equipment, and dashed headlong across the fields toward the road and orchard at a full gallop. Major James Dearing, who was riding ahead of his battalion, accompanied this rush. A new offensive line was soon established by these six batteries at and contiguous to Sherfy's peach orchard from which a second bombardment of the Federal forces was initiated and maintained until Barksdale was driven back. General Barksdale was mortally wounded, and his Mississippi troops were pursued by Col. George L. Willard's New York Brigade. Willard's soldiers were checked by Huger's fire, and he was killed by it at Plum Run in Nicholas Codori's thicket. Many casualties resulted from this convergence of musket balls and cannon shells, one of which was Corp. Joseph Lantz. While crossing the fields between Seminary Ridge and the shell-smashed orchard, Lantz, a member of Capt. Osmond Taylor's "Bath" Virginia Battery, was struck by a missile which broke both thighs causing his death within minutes. At that moment he called out: "You can do me no good; I am killed; follow your piece."

Cabell's Battalion for a short time previous to the advance of Barksdale and Huger, had drawn concentrated barrages from Union batteries at the Peach Orchard and along the Emmitsburg Road, while simultaneously receiving a destructive pummeling on their flank from Lt. Charles E. Hazlett's 5th "Regulars" on Little Round Top. This combined shelling was so incessant that it became necessary at times to cease firing to allow the smoke to clear away. The harm to officers and men was acute, including Capt. John Fraser and Lt. R.H. Couper seriously wounded, plus two sergeants killed and a private injured by the explosion of the same projectile. This Georgia battery was so crippled that its 3-inch rifles were sent to Capt. Manly's Battery. When the fighting here ended, Fraser's two rifles, and his pair of 10-pounder Parrotts, in addition to a couple of rifles from Edward McCarthy's Battery, were arranged in three sections and began to prepare for what was to come on the morrow. This new forward alignment was under the leadership of Lieutenants J.H. Payne, R.M. Anderson and William J. Furlong, respectively.

Major Benjamin Eshleman's Battalion, which had been in reserve, was brought up in the evening. However they saw no active duty, as the area combat had faded by the time they reached Pitzer's schoolhouse. Some harassing artillery fire continued until darkness covered the field, which someone said, made, "the fuses of the flying shells look like meteors in the sky."

It was a busy night for the artillerymen of both sides. The dead were hurriedly buried, and the many wounded were collected and removed to field hospitals in the rear. Caissons and limbers rumbled back to the supply trains, while the drivers brought up sound horses, taken from wagons, and the much lightened ammunition vehicles, to replace those killed and disabled. Amidst these important chores, Col. Alexander caught a few hours of sleep on a bed of fence-rails. But around 3:00 A.M., he began the task of putting the serviceable guns of the three battalions under his command, into position for the demands expected of them on

Colonel Edward P. Alexander

July 3. Considering the important activities and responsibilities thrust upon him, it must be remembered that Alexander was not the actual leader of the First Corps' artillery arm.

General James Longstreet, writing after the war, commented on this very subject. "Our artillery was in charge of [Col.] Alexander, a brave and gifted officer. Colonel Walton was my chief of artillery; but Alexander, being at the head of the column, and being first in position, and being, beside, an officer of unusual promptness, sagacity and intelligence, was given charge of the artillery." Naturally, the friends of

Col. Walton resented this as an inferential injustice. Later, Gen. Longstreet was impelled to refine his earlier statement. "It is true that..., there were sentences subject to the erroneous impression that Colonel Walton was not in full command of the artillery of the First Corps at the battle of Gettysburg. My orders, however, as well as my instructions... were addressed to Colonel J.B. Walton as Chief of Artillery, and show conclusively he was in command on that day. Colonel Alexander figured more prominently in the correspondence that passed between myself and the artillery, simply because I had consulted personally with Colonel Alexander on these points before the battle opened, and because he was most directly interested in the handling of the artillery massed at the peach orchard, and under cover of which Pickett was to make his charge. Colonel Walton was a brave and capable officer, and I regret that my narrative was so construed as to reflect upon his fair and spotless record."

The Horse Artillery

The brigade of artillery attached to Gen. Stuart's Cavalry Division was composed of four Virginia, one Maryland, and one South Carolina batteries. Four of these batteries operated with Gen. Stuart's column, and three of them, Capt. James Breathed, (VA), Capt. William M. McGregor, (VA), and Capt. Thomas E. Jackson, (VA), reinforced by the Parrott section of Capt. Charles A. Green's (LA) Battery, of Hilary P. Jones' Battalion, participated in Stuart's afternoon cavalry fight with Gen. David Gregg's troopers east of Gettysburg on July 3. The remaining two batteries accompanied the cavalry brigades of Gen. Beverly H. Robertson and Gen. William E. Jones, which in late June had been left south of the Potomac, but rejoined Lee's army in time to aid in covering the retreat.

Pickett's Charge

After a post-dawn change of plans, Gen. Robert E. Lee became determined to assault Cemetery Ridge on Friday July 3 with several brigades from Hill's and Longstreet's infantry corps, using as a spearhead, three fresh units from the division of Maj. Gen. George E. Pickett. The new directives for this attack were issued to Col. Alexander by Gen. Longstreet around 9:00 A.M., and necessitated the shifting and realignment of his 75 cannon. These changes fell under the watchful eye of the Federal gunners, whose fluttering guidons could be seen skimming along just above the crest of the rolling swales and ridges to the east. Fortunately, the modifications called for were accomplished quietly and inoffensively, thus avoiding the attention of the Yankees, who, had they known the situation, might have commenced fire before the errors were rectified.

Several hours earlier, Gen. Cadmus M. Wilcox's Brigade, of Richard H. Anderson's Division, had joined Alexander's growing covey of guns. His brigade was deployed parallel with the Emmitsburg Road and about 200 yards to the west of it, with   Alexander's field pieces extending far beyond either flank in Wilcox's front. The three regiments of Col. David Lang's Florida Brigade were placed on the left of Wilcox's Georgians. Wilcox and Lang remained in this locale until about 3:20 P.M., at that time they were hurried toward the enemy on Cemetery Ridge to provide support for Pickett's right flank.

Along Seminary Ridge to the left of Alexander's 75 pieces, and on a track beginning six hundred yards in his rear, were sixty-three additional cannon belonging to Gen. A.P. Hill's Corps, and supervised by Col. R. Lindsay Walker. These batteries would oversee the left assaulting divisions directed by Generals James J. Pettigrew and Isaac R. Trimble, and consisting of six brigades then commanded by Col. Birkett D. Fry, Col. James K. Marshall, Gen. Joseph R. Davis, Col. Robert M. Mayo, Col. William L.J. Lowrance, and Gen. James H. Lane. Overall then, including the above units and the five brigades of Pickett, Lang and Wilcox, there would be no more than 12,000 infantrymen committed to this effort. In addition, as the firing distance from Seminary Ridge to the Federal forces was too great for them, Gen. Pendleton offered Alexander nine howitzers belonging to the Third Corps. This proposal was gladly accepted, and these short-range weapons were pulled into a hollow behind Seminary Ridge, where they were to remain until sent for.

By the time these many ongoing preparations were completed, the artillery heads of the three Confederate corps, Colonels Edward Alexander, J. Thompson Brown, and R. Lindsay Walker, had at their disposal between 170 and 179 guns with which to bombard Gen. Meade's army prior to the afternoon assault.

Alexander's own formation, as arranged to cover his part of the infantry attack, began at the Peach Orchard with Cabell's Battalion. Captain Basil C. Manly's (NC) Battery, now increased to three sections, by pieces from Fraser's (GA) and McCarthy's (VA) commands, were posted on the right near the John and Mary Wentz house which stood within Sherfy's orchard. The remaining section of McCarthy's Battery, (two Napoleons), with Henry Carlton's (GA) Battery, were sent to the extreme left, and, owing to the conformation of the ground, was placed *en echelon* to the regular order of battle.

Next in the configuration came Alexander's own battalion, under his close friend and comrade, Maj. Frank Huger. The batteries of Captains Tyler C. Jordan, (VA), George V. Moody, (LA), William W. Parker, (VA), and Osmond B. Taylor, (VA), filled out the ranks from Sherfy's farm buildings and generally northward, following the course of the Emmitsburg Road to the David Klingel house in the order named. Lieutenant S. Capers Gilbert's "Brooks Artillery", (SC), and Lt. James Woolfolk's (VA) Battery, (Capt. Woolfolk was injured on July 2), were delegated to the extreme left of the aforementioned units and arranged *en echelon* and somewhat in rear of the left of Alexander's sector, and in front of the right of Hill's guns on Seminary Ridge.

Major B.F. Eshleman's Battalion, the Washington Artillery, followed next, employing eight Napoleons and two 12-pounder howitzers. Captain Merritt B. Miller's four 12-pounder Napoleons were set on the highest piece of terrain at the junction of Henry Spangler's farm lane and the Emmitsburg Road to the left of O.B. Taylor's Battery. Captain Joseph Norcom's company, (two Napoleons), was unlimbered on Miller's left; Capt. John B. Richardson, with the remaining two pieces filled out the line. Two howitzers were kept as a reserve, and overseen by Lt. George E. Apps. In considering the alterations made from the original dispositions after sunrise, we see Norcom and Richardson moved to the left and rear, and formed *en echelon* by batteries, and the five guns of Cabell's Battalion, (Carlton and McCarthy) shifted to the north, or left, and wedged between the two Louisiana companies.

During the forenoon, Captains Taylor and Miller threw a few rounds into the Yankee skirmish line, drawing some return shots from Cemetery Ridge. Before Capt. Richardson went to the left, he noticed a 3-inch rifle, abandoned previously by Capt. James Thompson, (C & F, PA), in a field between the contending armies, about 300 yards out from the Northern pickets. Privates William Forrest and Jim Brown, two drivers of Richardson's Second Company, Washington Artillery, successfully brought off the piece under a heavy fire from enemy riflemen. The accompanying limber contained about 50 rounds of ammunition, which was used irreverently, in the captured gun, against its own soldiers that very afternoon.

Major James Dearing directed the artillery coordinating with Gen. George Pickett's Division. His battalion marched onto the battlefield early on the morning of July 3, and several hours afterward was emplaced as

A section of the Confederate artillery line placed along Emmitsburg Road in preparation for Pickett's charge on July 3.

follows: Capt. Robert M. Stribling, (VA), Capt. Miles C. Macon, (VA), Capt. William H. Caskie, (VA), and Capt. Joseph G. Blount, (VA), were added to Alexander's force northward, on ground in a generally east-west line, from Peter Rogers' house, over to the ripple of high land west of David Klingle's barn. This placed Dearing on the left of Eshleman's Battalion, and in front of the point to be assaulted, with part of Cabell's Battalion on their left rear. This battalion also encountered U.S. infantrymen during the forenoon, and had several men and horses hit by their fire. Major John P.W. Read, who was superintending Stribling's Battery during the forenoon, was struck by a shell fragment and badly injured.

Between 10:00 A.M. and noon, intense and heavy skirmishing occurred around the William and Adeline Bliss farm west of Zeigler's Grove, which lay on the northern end of Cemetery Ridge. This fighting involved the useless expenditure of much of Gen. Hill's valuable ammunition. When this affair was over, and the fighting at Culp's Hill had been decided with the withdrawal of Gen. Ewell's Confederates to Rock Creek, the fields, orchards, and meadows between Cemetery and

> *An average Union light-artillery battery of 12-pounder Napoleons, at full strength, contained six guns and carriages, 91 horses, 12 limbers, six caissons, one battery wagon, and one forge wagon; also one captain, four lieutenants, and 150 enlisted men, which included eight sergeants, 12 corporals, 52 drivers, 70 cannoneers, six artificers, and two buglers.*

Seminary Ridges presented a peaceful contrast to the mad whirl that would follow after mid-day.

About noonday Col. Alexander rode to the left of his artillery line to observe the effect of his fire, and when the favorable moment arrived, give, as instructed by Gen. Longstreet, the order for Pickett's Division to begin the advance. Strangely and unaccountably, the correspondence that ensued prior to the start of the cannonade, between Gen. Longstreet and Col. Alexander, fixed the decision and responsibility on whether to attack or not, squarely on the shoulders of Alexander. Alexander was a mere colonel who was not the chief of artillery for Lee's army, nor was he in fact, even the head of that branch in Longstreet's Corps. It appears, in retrospect, both officers were torn by doubt that the undertaking could succeed; therefore there was a hesitation to issue orders which would send hundreds of brave men in a useless sacrifice of their lives.

Altogether several written and verbal messages passed between the two officers on that fateful day. Though confused, and uncertain of such a grave encumbrance, Alexander, in one communication, did consent to Longstreet's wishes, saying: "When our Arty. fire is at its best I will advise Gen. Pickett to advance." Soon thereafter Alexander sent for the howitzers proffered by Gen. Pendleton, only to find that Pendleton had, himself, taken a part of the detachment, and the others had been moved away for reasons of safety. It was Alexander's intention to have these howitzers accompany Pickett's regiments to within musket range.

At approximately 1:00 P.M. Longstreet sent these instructions to James B. Walton, his artillery chief: "Colonel: Let the batteries open. Order great care and precision in firing. If the batteries at the Peach Orchard cannot be used against the point we intend attacking, let them open on the enemy on the rocky-hill." [Little Round Top]

This order was communicated to Maj. Eshleman, and a moment later a red tongue of flame leaped from the mouth of one of Capt. Miller's Napoleons, which was followed shortly by a second detonation. With this signal the afternoon battle was joined and for almost two hours the cannonading on both sides, like rolling thunder, was more or less continuous and incessant. During this bombardment, which was replied to by about 80 Federal cannon according to Gen. Hunt, the waiting foot soldiers of Pickett and Pettigrew suffered considerably, though somewhat out-of-sight and protected. For examples, Gen. Richard B. Garnett's Brigade had nearly 20 killed and wounded, including Lt. Col. John T. Ellis, 19th Virginia, who was decapitated. In Company G, of the 11th Virginia, Gen. James L. Kemper's right regiment, three men were killed and seven injured, out of 29 present for duty. And Company E, on the right of G, had a still larger number hit. Artillery casualties also mounted steadily, as thousands of shrieking projectiles fell from the sky. Lieutenant Henry Jennings and Capt. Henry H. Carlton, of Cabell's Battalion, were badly hurt while discharging their duties and Maj. Eshleman saw Capt. Joseph Norcom fall early in the contest when he was struck by a shell fragment. The command of Norcom's Battery devolved upon Lt. H.A. Battles. Other losses included Lieutenants S. Capers Gilbert, Charles H.C. Brown, and George Apps, all of the Washington Artillery, plus Maj. John Read, of Dearing's Battalion, as previously noted.

Weapons, battery vehicles, equipment, and horses took a beating too, as the iron rain of shot and shell plummeted to the earth from above. Lieutenant Battles, of Norcom's Battery had two pieces disabled. Captain Miller's loss in horses was so great that he could maneuver only one piece. The rifle captured earlier and brought off by Capt. John Richardson was the victim of a Yankee solid shot and put out of commission.

After the artillery duel had been in progress for nearly 40 minutes, a courier brought a dispatch to Gen. Pickett from Col. Alexander, which, after reading, he handed to Gen. Longstreet. It stated: "If you are coming at all, you must come at once, or I cannot give you proper support, but the enemy's fire has not slackened at all. At least 18 guns are still firing from the cemetery itself." Pickett turned and asked, "General, shall I advance?" Longstreet merely bowed his head affirmatively, afraid to speak, as he later recounted, lest he might betray to his subordinate, his want of confidence in the assault. As Longstreet mounted to join Alexander, Pickett saluted and said, "I shall lead my division forward, sir."

When his corps commander arrived, Alexander related the incident of the disappearance of the howitzers, which were to have accompanied Pickett, and the fact that ammunition was so low that the attack could not be properly supported; to replenish, he warned, would take an hour. Even without this bad news, Longstreet, still wanted Pickett stopped. The order to do so however was never given.

As the cannonade slackened and eventually ceased altogether, and the dense smoke of battle began to clear away, Longstreet and Alexander strained to catch a glimpse of Pickett's approaching troops. Soon a courier galloped up to Gen. Lewis A. Armistead, who was on foot pacing up and down in front of his regiment of direction, the 53rd Virginia. The order had come! As Gen. Richard Garnett's Brigade began to move out, Armistead called out his commands over the slowly receding noise of the cannonade: "Attention, battalion!" And then, "Right shoulder, shift arms, Forward, March." Now the compact lines of Pickett's three brigades began to move steadily and resolutely forward through the file of still hot, smoking Southern guns. These determined Virginians, in conjunction with Pettigrew's Brigades on the far left, soon made their way to, and then across the Emmitsburg Road, where the tight, neatly dressed ranks of human bodies were torn and broken by a deadly hail of shot, shell, and canister. On up the gentle slope of Cemetery Ridge they staggered, full in the face of the concentrated firepower of the powder-blackened cannon spurting flaming death at point-blank range, and the blue-coated infantrymen on the crest throwing solid sheets of musketry volleys into the already bleeding and disorganized companies.

Years after the war, Gen. Longstreet wrote of the sad scene: "When the smoke cleared away, Pickett's Division was gone." By this, of course, he did not mean that Pickett's troops had faltered or fled, for over one-half of those men lay dead, dying, or wounded on the field. But simply, they, and the fortunate survivors who sullenly re-crossed the combat-scarred ground to safety behind Seminary Ridge, had faced a destructive fire that no soldiers, "ever arrayed for battle" could have withstood.

On Gen. Pickett's left, the story was the same. All six brigades committed to the undertaking by Gen. Ambrose Hill, had advanced just as bravely to Cemetery Ridge. Composed of many veteran riflemen from the states of North Carolina, Alabama, Mississippi, Tennessee, and Virginia, these units were equally wrecked by the formidable and furious defensive shown by Federal riflemen of Gen. Winfield S. Hancock's Second Corps. On this flank too, the Confederates lucky enough to be left standing,

---

Between 1861 and 1865 the Federal government bought 5,748,462 artillery projectiles and 9,540,603 pounds of cannon powder.

The DuPont Powder Mill in Delaware, one of 14 suppliers of gunpowder, could produce 175 barrels a day.

quickly sought shelter behind the far, green ridge. The Herculean task had been too much for the naked valor of the infantry. Robert E. Lee's "long arm" was not potent enough to enable the common soldier to carry the day. Either way, and for all concerned, at that moment the Battle of Gettysburg had been either lost or won.

When the repulse became apparent, Longstreet sent staff officers to assist in rallying the confused and disintegrating fragments of the retreating regiments and, with Alexander, hurried to the site where the batteries still remained at rest but steady. Upon arrival, his eyes took in an interesting and soothing spectacle. "As I rode along the line of artillery, I observed my old friend Captain Miller, Washington artillery,... walking between his guns and smoking his pipe as quietly and contentedly as he would at his camp-fire."

Now that the infantry had retreated, it was imperative for the artillery to check any enemy counter-stroke, and Maj. Benjamin Eshleman's Battalion was in the best location to accomplish this mission. Alexander's Battalion and that of Col. Henry Cabell were in their original deployments along the Emmitsburg Road between the Peach Orchard and Klingel's house, on Eshleman's right. The section of McCarthy's Battery, and three guns of Carlton's Battery under Lt. C.W. Motes, were run forward to a point near the road, west of the Codori farm structures, on Eshleman's left. The batteries of Captains George Ward, (MS), and James V. Brooke, (VA), plus Lt. Woolfolk, (VA), were still sitting,

One of Poague's howitzers in an earthen lunette on Seminary Ridge

en echelon, on the left of Alexander's line. Woolfolk was at the northeast corner of Spangler's woods, and Ward and Brooke were nearly 500 yards west of Codori's house, with Gen. Wright's Georgia Brigade pushed out for their support. General Hill's Third Corps pieces were intact on Seminary Ridge, with Lt. Col. John Garnett's Battalion and William Poague's howitzers in reserve. The rifled cannon of Capt. Willis Dance's Battalion at the Seminary covered, with a flanking sweep, the fields over which a counter-attack could have been made.

It should be remembered that only four of the eleven brigades that participated in Longstreet's assault on July 3 were detached from Gen. Lee's main tactical line, and that the Confederate batteries had expended very little of their canister rounds. This knowledge should be pondered by those disposed to criticize army commander Gen. George G. Meade for not having rushed forth and marshaled Northern forces for his own assault against the Rebels on Seminary Ridge.

The Retreat

In the aftermath of Longstreet's disastrous and failed attack, the Confederate army was obliged to assume defensive measures late on the third day and into Saturday, July 4. All artillery was withdrawn from its advanced offensive positions, and the troops and guns on Seminary Ridge were held ready for any emergency. Major Charles Richardson with five rifles from Garnett's Battalion, Maj. Eshleman with seven 12-pounders and one 3-inch rifle, and Capt. William A. Tanner with four cannons from Jones' Battalion, and a Whitworth gun, were detailed to Gen. John D. Imboden's mounted brigade at Cashtown to aid in the escort of the wounded and other trains in the general retreat to Williamsport, MD. Imboden was also joined by Capt. James F. Hart, (SC), a four-gun battery from Gen. James E.B. Stuart's horse-artillery brigade, which, with the six guns of his own battery, led by Capt. John H. McClanahan, (VA), gave Imboden ample fire power for the protection of the wagon and ambulance trains.

On July 7 the artillery, with the main body of the army, encamped near Hagerstown. The total loss in officers and men in the Gettysburg Campaign was 94 killed, 437 wounded, and 77 missing. The monthly returns for July (after Gettysburg), indicate 277 officers and 4,736 men present for duty. This sum of 5,013 officers and enlisted men, to which, if added the 608 casualties of the campaign, (exclusive of Stuart's horse artillery), makes the strength of the Confederate artillery force, in the

Army of Northern Virginia at Gettysburg, 5,621 soldiers (with between 278 and 283 guns).

Two guns of Capt. John W. Lewis' Virginia Battery fell into the hands of Gen. Judson Kilpatrick's U.S. cavalry division on July 14 at Falling Waters, MD, and became the subject of supplemental reports filed by Generals Meade and Lee to their respective chiefs. Lee claimed that the weapons had been left in the road, due to the battery horses being completely exhausted, while officers went out to procure others. Supposedly, before they could return, the rear of the column had passed the guns making it unsafe to even attempt to bring them off. General Meade, in his reference to Lee's version, enclosed Kilpatrick's personal view of the affair, in which he made these disclosures:

> Learning from citizens that a portion of the enemy had retreated in the direction of Falling Waters, I at once moved rapidly for that point, and came up with the rear guard of the enemy at 7:30 a.m., at a point 2 miles distant from Falling Waters. We pressed on, driving them before us, capturing many prisoners and one gun. When within a mile and a half of Falling Waters, the enemy was found in large force, drawn up in line of battle, on the crest of a hill commanding the road on which I was advancing.... Within less than 1,000 yards of this large force, a second piece of artillery with its support (consisting of infantry) was captured while attempting to get into position. The gun was taken to the rear.

General Lee's report conveys the impression that no organized body of his men had been captured at this time; only stragglers and others who had been left asleep in the houses and barns along the route of march. Meade, in his reply to this suggestion, responded: "The three battle-flags captured on this occasion and sent to Washington belonged to the 40th, 47th and 55th Virginia Regiments (infantry). General Lee will surely acknowledge these were not left in the hands of 'stragglers asleep in barns.'"

The day of the Gettysburg artillery is past. The guns are all silent now, and stand only to enhance the "war scenery" throughout the battlefield park, as they quietly mark the various battery positions here and there across the once bitterly contested landscape. The brave, powder-begrimed and sweat-drenched artillerymen who served the brooding Napoleons, rifles, and howitzers, are long dead. Memories of them too, are fast receding. If we are not careful, little of what they did at Gettysburg or elsewhere will matter to the growing population of a busy and self-absorbed planet. Our modern, crowded world seems even now to have small use for such abstract events. It remains for us who are dedicated to the preservation of the important world altering events of that history, as well as the hallowed places where it occurred, to save the stories, the memories and the battlegrounds of those men and deeds which we today so cherish and remember.[11]

Limbers and caissons parked on the backside of CemeteryRidge

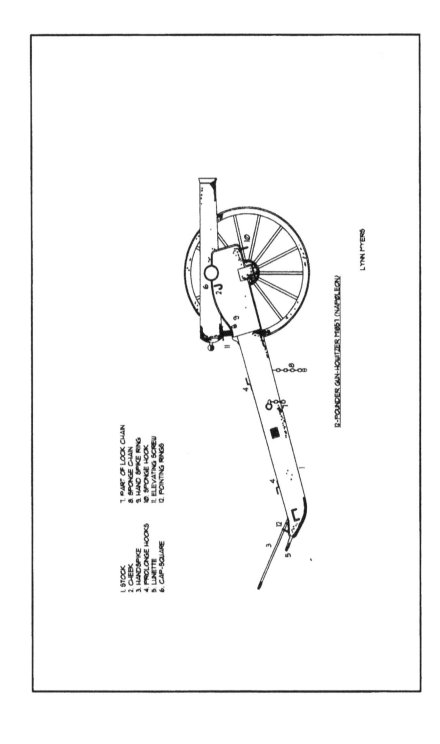

1. STOCK
2. CHEEK
3. HANDSPIKE
4. PROLONGE HOOKS
5. LUNETTE
6. CAP-SQUARE

7. PART OF LOCK CHAIN
8. SPONGE CHAIN
9. HAND SPIKE RING
10. SPONGE HOOK
11. ELEVATING SCREW
12. POINTING RINGS

12-POUNDER GUN-HOWITZER M1857 (NAPOLEON)

LYNN MYERS

The Union Artillery Units at Gettysburg

Their Armaments, Strengths and Casualties

The following list is compiled to indicate the complete name of all Northern batteries, their commanders, guns employed, the muster on June 30, 1863, and the losses incurred at Gettysburg. The number in parenthesis ( ) are men present in the battle; the three other figures represent, "killed," "wounded," and "missing/prisoners." A question mark means that no figures are available.

The Army of the Potomac
Gen. Henry J. Hunt, Chief of Artillery

First Corps Artillery Brigade, Col. Charles S. Wainwright

2nd Maine Light Artillery, (Battery B), Capt. James A. Hall
  6 – 3" rifles   (120)   0-18-0

5th Maine Light Artillery, (Battery E),
  Capt. Greenleaf T. Stevens, Lt. Edward N. Whittier
  6 - Napoleons   (128)   3-13-7

1st New York Light Artillery, Battery L,
  Capt. Gilbert A. Reynolds, Lt. Geo. Breck
  6 – 3" rifles   (133)   1-15-1

1st Pennsylvania Light Artillery, Battery B, Capt. James H. Cooper
  4 – 3" rifles   (114)   3-9-0

4th United States Artillery, Battery B, Lt. James Stewart
6 - Napoleons   (132)   2-31-3

Second Corps Artillery Brigade, Capt. John G. Hazard

1st New York Light Artillery, Battery B, (14th New York Battery
attached) Lt. Albert S. Sheldon, Capt. James M. Rorty, Lt.
Robert E. Rogers
4 - 10-pdr Parrotts   (122)   10-16-0

1st Rhode Island Light Artillery, Battery A, Capt. William A. Arnold
6 – 3" rifles   (126)   3-28-1

1st Rhode Island Light Artillery, Battery B, Lt. T. Fred. Brown,
Lt. Walter S. Perrin
6 - Napoleons   (139)   7-19-2

1st United States Artillery, Battery I, Lt. George A. Woodruff,
Lt. Tully McCrea
6 - Napoleons   (120)   1-24-0

4th United States Artillery, Battery A, Lt. Alonzo H. Cushing,
Sgt. Frederick Fuger
6 – 3" rifles   (136)   6-32-0

Third Corps Artillery Brigade, Capt. George E. Randolph,
Capt. A. Judson Clark

1st New Jersey Light Artillery, Battery B, (or Independent NJ
2nd Battery) Capt. A. Judson Clark, Lt. Robert Sims
6 - 10-pdr Parrotts   (141)   1-16-3

1st New York Light Artillery, Battery D, Capt. George B. Winslow
6 - Napoleons   (118)   0-10-8

4th New York Independent Battery, Capt. James E. Smith
6 - 10-pdr Parrotts   (135)   2-10-1

1st Rhode Island Light Artillery, Battery E, Lt. John K. Bucklyn, Lt.
Benjamin Freeborn
6 - Napoleons   (116)   3-26-1

4th United States Artillery, Battery K, Lt. Francis W. Seeley,
Lt. Robert James
6 - Napoleons   (121)   2-19-4

Fifth Corps Artillery Brigade, Capt. Augustus P. Martin

3rd Massachusetts Light Artillery, (Battery C), Lt. Aaron F. Walcott
6 - Napoleons   (124)   0-6-0

1st New York Light Artillery, Battery C, Capt. Almont Barnes
4 – 3" rifles   (88)   0-0-0

1st Ohio Light Artillery, Battery L, Capt. Frank C. Gibbs
6 - Napoleons   (121)   0-2-0

5th United States Artillery, Battery D, Lt. Charles E. Hazlett,
Lt. Benjamin F. Rittenhouse
6 - 10-pdr Parrotts   (73)   7-6-0

5th United States Artillery, Battery I, Lt. Malbone F. Watson,
Lt. Charles C. MacConnell
4 – 3" rifles   (76)   1-19-2

Sixth Corps Artillery Brigade, Col. Charles H. Tompkins

1st Massachusetts Light Artillery, (Battery A), Capt. William H.
McCartney
6 - Napoleons   (145)   0-0-0

1st New York Independent Battery, Capt. Andrew Cowan
6 – 3" rifles   (111)   4-8-0

3rd New York Independent Battery, Capt. William A. Harn
6 - 10-pdr Parrotts   (119)   0-0-0

1st Rhode Island Light Artillery, Battery C, Capt. Richard Waterman
6 – 3" rifles   (125)   0-0-0

1st Rhode Island Light Artillery, Battery G, Capt. George A. Adams
6 - 10-pdr Parrotts   (135)   0-0-0

2nd United States Artillery, Battery D, Lt. Edward B. Williston
6 - Napoleons   (135)   0-0-0

2nd United States Artillery, Battery G, Lt. John H. Butler
6 - Napoleons   (109)   0-0-0

5th United States Artillery, Battery F, Lt. Leonard Martin
6 - 10-pdr Parrotts   (125)   0-0-0

Eleventh Corps Artillery Brigade, Maj. Thomas W. Osborn

1st New York Light Artillery, Battery I, Capt. Michael Wiedrich
6 – 3" rifles   (146)   3-10-0

13th New York Independent Battery, Lt. William Wheeler
4 – 3" rifles   (118)   0-8-3

1st Ohio Light Artillery, Battery I, Capt. Hubert Dilger
6 - Napoleons   (137)   0-13-0

1st Ohio Light Artillery, Battery K, Capt. Lewis Heckman
4 - Napoleons   (118)   2-11-2

4th United States Artillery, Battery G, Lt. Bayard Wilkeson,
Lt. Eugene A. Bancroft
6 - Napoleons   (124)   2-11-4

Twelfth Corps Artillery Brigade, Lt. Edward D. Muhlenberg

1st New York Light Artillery, Battery M, Lt. Charles E. Winegar
4 - 10-pdr Parrotts   (97)   0-0-0

Pennsylvania Independent Battery E, Lt. Charles A. Atwell
6 - 10-pdr Parrotts   (127)   0-3-0

4th United States Artillery, Battery F, Lt. Sylvanus T. Rugg
  6 - Napoleons   (96)   0-1-0

5th United States Artillery, Battery K, Lt. David H. Kinzie
  4 - Napoleons   (77)   0-5-0

Cavalry Corps

Horse Artillery, First Brigade, Capt. James M. Robertson

9th Michigan Battery, (1st Michigan Artillery, Battery I), Capt.
      Jabez J. Daniels
  6 – 3" rifles   (119)   1-4-0

6th New York Independent Battery, Capt. Joseph W. Martin
  6 – 3" rifles   (111)   0-1-0

2nd United States Artillery, Batteries B and L, Lt. Edward Heaton
  6 – 3" rifles   (106)   0-0-0

2nd United States Artillery, Battery M, Lt. Alexander C.M.
      Pennington, Jr.
  6 – 3" rifles   (129)   0-1-0

4th United States Artillery, Battery E, Lt. Samuel S. Elder
  4 – 3" rifles   (66)   1-0-0

3rd Pennsylvania Heavy Artillery, Battery H, Capt. William D. Rank
  2 – 3" rifles   (55)   0-1-0
  (*This unit was detached and served as light artillery with Col.
  John B. McIntosh's brigade of cavalry for a short time, except on
  July 3 when it was on Cemetery Ridge.*)

Horse Artillery, Second Brigade, Capt. John C. Tidball

1st United States Artillery, Batteries E and G, Capt. Alanson M.
      Randol
  4 – 3" rifles   (91)   0-0-0

1st United States Artillery, Battery K, Capt. William M. Graham
  6 – 3" rifles   (123)   2-1-0

2nd United States Artillery, Battery A, Lt. John H. Calef
6 – 3" rifles   (81)   0-12-0

Artillery Reserve, Gen. Robert O. Tyler, Capt. James M. Robertson

First Regular Brigade, Capt. Dunbar R. Ransom

1st United States Artillery, Battery H, Lt. Chandler P. Eakin,
Lt. Philip D. Mason
6 - Napoleons   (153)   1-8-1

3rd United States Artillery, Batteries F and K,
Lt. John G. Turnbull
6 - Napoleons   (136)   9-14-1

4th United States Artillery, Battery C, Lt. Evan Thomas
6 - Napoleons   (113)   1-17-0

5th United States Artillery, Battery C, Lt. Gulian V. Weir
6 - Napoleons   (123)   2-14-0

First Volunteer Brigade, Lt. Col. Freeman McGilvery

5th Massachusetts Light Artillery, (Battery F),
Capt. Charles A. Phillips
6 – 3" rifles   (115)   4-17-0

9th Massachusetts Light Artillery, Capt. John Bigelow,
Lt. Richard S. Milton
6 - Napoleons   (110)   8-18-2

15th New York Independent Battery, Capt. Patrick Hart
4 - Napoleons   (102)   3-13-0

Pennsylvania Independent Batteries C and F, Capt. James Thompson
6 – 3" rifles   (118)   2-23-3

Second Volunteer Brigade, Capt. Elijah D. Taft

1st Connecticut Heavy Artillery, Battery B, Capt. Albert F. Brooker
  (*left behind in Westminster, MD as train guards*)
  6 - 4.5" rifles (110)   0-0-0

1st Connecticut Heavy Artillery, Battery M, Capt Franklin A. Pratt
  (*left behind in Westminster, MD as train guards*)
  6 - 4.5" rifles (110)   0-0-0

2nd Connecticut Light Artillery, Independent Battery,
      Capt. John W. Sterling
      4 - James rifles (110)   0-3-2
      2 - 12-pdr howitzers

5th New York Independent Battery, Capt. Elijah D. Taft
      6 - 20-pdr Parrotts   (162)   1-2-0

Third Volunteer Brigade, Capt. James F. Huntington

1st New Hampshire Light Artillery, (Battery A),
      Capt. Frederick M. Edgell
      4 – 3" rifles   (102)   0-3-0

1st Ohio Light Artillery, Battery H, Lt. George W. Norton
      6 - 3" rifles   (117)   2-5-0

1st Pennsylvania Light Artillery, Batteries F and G,
      Capt. R. Bruce Ricketts
      6 – 3" rifles   (165)   6-14-3

1st West Virginia Light Artillery, Battery C,
      Capt. Wallace Hill
      4 - 10 pdr Parrotts   (118)   2-2-0

Fourth Volunteer Brigade, Capt. Robert H. Fitzhugh

6th Maine Light Artillery, Battery F, Lt. Edwin B. Dow
      4 - Napoleons (103)   0-13-0

1st Maryland Light Artillery, Battery A, Capt. James H. Rigby
   6 – 3" rifles   (113)   0-0-0

1st New Jersey Light Artillery, Battery A, Lt. Augustin N. Parsons
   6 - 10-pdr Parrotts   (116)   2-7-0

1st New York Light Artillery, Battery G, Capt. Nelson Ames
   6 - Napoleons   (138)   0-7-0

1st New York Light Artillery, Battery K, (11th New York
   Independent Battery attached) Capt. Robert H. Fitzhugh
   6 – 3" rifles   (145)   0-7-0

Total, Gettysburg Campaign

          358-372 guns in 67 batteries
          about 7,500 men
          8,400 horses
          358-372 caissons
          862 limbers
          67 traveling forge wagons, and 67 battery wagons
     Losses: (at Gettysburg)
          110 killed, 595 wounded, 54 missing and prisoners, total 759

The Union army probably captured only about five cannons from
Confederate forces during the campaign.[12]

The Confederate Artillery Units at Gettysburg

Their Armaments, Strengths and Casualties

The following list is compiled to indicate the complete name of all Southern batteries, their commanders, guns employed, the muster on June 30, 1863, and the losses incurred at Gettysburg. The number in parenthesis ( ) are men present in the battle; the three other figures represent, "killed," "wounded," and "missing/prisoners." The question mark (?) denotes that no information is available.

The Army of Northern Virginia
Gen. William N. Pendleton, Chief of Artillery

First Corps, Col. James B. Walton, Chief of Artillery

McLaw's Division Artillery Battalion, Col. Henry C. Cabell

Carlton's (Georgia) Battery (Troup Artillery)
      Capt. Henry H. Carlton, Lt. C. W. Motes
      2 - 12-pdr howitzers   (95)   2-5-0
      2 - 10-pdr Parrotts

Fraser's (Georgia) Battery (Pulaski Artillery) Capt. John C. Fraser,
      Lt. William J. Furlong
      2 – 3" rifles   (67)   7-12-0
      2 - 10-pdr Parrotts

McCarthy's (Virginia) Battery (First Richmond Howitzers)
      Capt. Edward S. McCarthy
      2 - Napoleons   (95)   3-10-0
      2 – 3" rifles

Manly's (North Carolina) Battery (First North Carolina Artillery, Battery
 A), Capt. Basil C. Manly
  2 - 12-pdr howitzers (139) 3-10-0
  2 - 10-pdr Parrotts

Pickett's Division Artillery Battalion, Maj. James Dearing

Blount's (Virginia) Battery, Capt. Joseph G. Blount
  4 - Napoleons (102) 5-3-2

Caskie's (Virginia) Battery, (Hampden Light Artillery),
  Capt. William H. Caskie
  2 - Napoleons (95)   0-3-0
  1 – 3" rifle
  1 - 10-pdr Parrott

Macon's (Virginia) Battery, (Richmond Fayette Light Artillery),
  Capt. Miles C. Macon
  2 - Napoleons (95) 3-1-1
  2 - 10-pdr Parrotts

  Stribling's (Virginia) Battery, (Fauquier Artillery),
  Capt. Robert M. Stribling
  4 - Napoleons (142) 1-4-0
  2 - 20-pdr Parrotts

Hood's Division Artillery Battalion, Maj. Mathis W. Henry and
 Maj. John C. Haskell

Bachman's (South Carolina) Battery, (German Artillery),
  Capt. William K. Bachman
4 - Napoleons (75) ?-?-?

Garden's (South Carolina) Battery, (Palmetto Light Artillery),
  Capt. Hugh R. Garden
  2 - Napoleons (67) 2-5-0
  2 - 10-pdr Parrotts

Latham's (North Carolina) Battery, (Bravely Artillery),
  Capt. Alexander C. Latham
  1 - 6-pdr field gun   (119)   1-2-0
  1 - 12-pdr howitzer
  3 - Napoleons

Reilly's (North Carolina) Battery, (Rowan Artillery),
  Capt. James Reilly
  2 - Napoleons   (157)   2-4-0
  2 – 3" rifles
  2 - 10-pdr Parrotts

Reserve Artillery, Col. James B. Walton

Edward P. Alexander's Battalion, Maj. Frank Huger

Jordan's (Virginia) Battery, (Bedford Artillery), Capt. Tyler C. Jordan
  4 – 3" rifles   (83)   1-7-1

Moody's (Louisiana) Battery, (Madison Light Artillery),
  Capt. George V. Moody
  4 - 24-pdr howitzers   (143)   4-29-0

Parker's (Virginia) Battery, Capt. William W. Parker
  3 – 3" rifles   (95)   3-14-1
  1 - 10-pdr Parrott

Gilbert's (South Carolina)Battery, [A.B. Rhett's] (Brooks Light Artillery),
  Lt. S. Capers Gilbert
  4 - 12-pdr howitzers   (76)   7-29-0

Taylor's (Virginia) Battery, (Bath Artillery), Capt. Osmond B. Taylor
  4 - Napoleons   (95)   4-8-1

Woolfolk's (Virginia) Battery, (Ashland Artillery),
  Capt. Pichegru Woolfolk, Jr., Lt. James Woolfolk
  2 - Napoleons   (109)   3-24-1
  2 - 20-pdr Parrotts

Washington (Louisiana) Artillery Battalion,
Maj. Benjamin F. Eshleman

1st Company (Brown's),[Squires'], Lt. Charles H.C. Brown,
    Capt. Charles W. Squires
    1 - Napoleon   (82)   1-0-3

2nd Company, Capt. John B. Richardson
    2 - Napoleons   (85)   2-3-1
    1 - 12-pdr howitzer

3rd Company, Capt. Merritt B. Miller
    3 - Napoleons   (98)   5-2-3

4th Company, Capt. Joseph Norcom, Lt. H.A. Battles
    2 - Napoleons   (85)   0-6-4
    1 - 12-pdr howitzer

Second Corps, Col. J. Thompson Brown, Chief of Artillery

Early's Division Artillery Battalion, Lt. Col. Hilary P. Jones

Carrington's (Virginia) Battery, (Charlottesville Artillery),
    Capt. James McD. Carrington
    4 - Napoleons   (75)   0-0-2

Garber's (Virginia) Battery, (Staunton Artillery),
    Capt. Asher W. Garber
    4 - Napoleons   (64)   0-1-0

Green's (Louisiana) Battery, (Louisiana Guard Artillery),
    Capt. Charles A. Green
    2 – 3" rifles   (64)   2-5-0
    2 - 10-pdr Parrotts

Tanner's (Virginia) Battery, (Courtney Artillery),
    Capt. William A. Tanner
    4 – 3" rifles   (95)   0-0-2

Johnson's Division Artillery Battalion, Lt. Col. R. Snowden Andrews, Maj. Joseph W. Latimer, Capt. Charles I. Raine

Brown's (Maryland) Battery, (Chesapeake Artillery),
    Capt. William D. Brown
    4 - 10-pdr Parrotts   (81)   8-9-0

Carpenter's (Virginia) Battery, (Alleghany Artillery),
    Capt. John C. Carpenter
    2 - Napoleons   (97)   10-14-0
    2 – 3" rifles

Dement's (Maryland) Battery, (First Maryland Battery),
    Capt. William F. Dement
    4 - Napoleons   (95)   1-4-0

Raine's (Virginia) Battery, (Lee Battery), Capt. Charles I. Raine,
    Lt. William W. Hardwicke
    1 – 3" rifle   (95)   2-2-0
    1 - 10-pdr Parrott
    2 - 20-pdr Parrotts

Rodes' Division Artillery Battalion, Lt. Col. Thomas H. Carter

Carter's (Virginia) Battery, (King William Artillery),
    Capt. William P. Carter
    2 - Napoleons   (109)   7-4-12
    2 - 10-pdr Parrotts

Fry's (Virginia) Battery, (Orange Artillery), Capt. Charles W. Fry
    2 – 3" rifles   (85)   0-0-7
    2 - 10-pdr Parrotts

Page's (Virginia) Battery, (Morris Artillery), Capt. Richard C.M. Page
    4 - Napoleons   (121)   7-25-7

Reese's (Alabama) Battery, (Jeff Davis Artillery), Capt. William J. Reese
    4 – 3" rifles   (84)   0-0-8

Reserve Artillery, Col. J. Thompson Brown

Capt. Willis J. Dance's Battalion (First Virginia Artillery)

Cunningham's (Virginia) Battery, (Powhatan Artillery),
    Lt. John M. Cunningham
    4 – 3" rifles   (83)   0-3-12

Griffin's (Virginia) Battery, [A. Hupp's] (Salem Artillery),
    Lt. Charles B. Griffin
    2 - Napoleons   (73)   0-2-5
    2 – 3" rifles

Graham's (Virginia) Battery, (Rockbridge Artillery),
    Capt. Archibald Graham
    4 - 20-pdr Parrotts   (90)   0-14-7

Smith's (Virginia) Battery, (3rd Richmond Howitzers),
    Capt. Benjamin H. Smith, Jr.
    4 – 3" rifles   (66)   1-1-2

Watson's (Virginia) Battery, (2nd Richmond Howitzers),
    Capt. David Watson
    4 - 10-pdr Parrotts   (68)   2-1-0

Lt. Col. William Nelson's Battalion

Kirkpatrick's (Virginia) Battery, (Amherst Artillery),
    Capt. Thomas J. Kirkpatrick
    3 - Napoleons   (112)   0-0-13
    1 – 3" rifle

Massie's (Virginia) Battery, (Fluvanna Artillery),
    Capt. John L. Massie
    3 - Napoleons   (95)   0-1-10
    1 – 3" rifle

Milledge's (Georgia) Battery, Capt. John Milledge, Jr.
    2 – 3" rifles   (77)   ?-?-?
    1 - 10-pdr Parrott

Third Corps, Col. R. Lindsay Walker, Chief of Artillery

Anderson's Division Artillery Battalion, (11th Georgia "Sumter" Artillery Battalion), Maj. John Lane

Company A (Ross') (Georgia) Capt. Hugh M. Ross or L.E. Spivey
    1 - 12-pdr howitzer   (138)   1-11-1
    1 - Napoleon
    1 – 3" navy rifle
    3 - 10-pdr Parrotts

Company B (Patterson's), (Georgia), Capt. George M. Patterson
    4 - 12-pdr howitzers   (132)   2-6-1
    2 - Napoleons

Company C (Wingfield's), (Georgia), Capt. John T. Wingfield
    3 – 3" navy rifles   (128)   0-18-2
    2 - 10-pdr Parrotts

Heth's Division Artillery Battalion, Lt. Col. John J. Garnett

Grandy's (Virginia) Battery, (Norfolk Light Artillery Blues),
    Capt. Charles R. Grandy
    2 - 12-pdr howitzers   (112)   0-1-1
    2 – 3" rifles

Lewis' (Virginia) Battery, (Pittsylvania Artillery), Capt. John W. Lewis
    2 - Napoleons   (95)   ?-?-?
    2 – 3" rifles

Maurin's (Louisiana) Battery, (Donaldsonville Artillery),
    Capt. Victor Maurin
    2 – 3" rifles   (121)   0-2-4
    1 - 10-pdr Parrott
Moore's (Virginia) Battery, Capt. Joseph D. Moore
    2 - Napoleons   (82)   ?-?-?
    1 – 3" rifle
    1 - 10-pdr Parrott

Pender's Division Artillery Battalion, Maj. William T. Poague

Brooke's (Virginia) Battery, (Warrenton Artillery),
    Capt. James V. Brooke
    2 - 12-pdr howitzers   (62)   1-2-2
    2 - Napoleons

Graham's (North Carolina) Battery, (Charlotte Artillery),
    Capt. Joseph Graham
    2 - 12-pdr howitzers   (133)   0-0-5
    2 - Napoleons

Ward's (Mississippi) Battery, (Madison Light Artillery),
    Capt. George Ward
    1 - 12-pdr howitzer   (97)   ?-?-?
    3 - Napoleons

Wyatt's (Virginia) Battery, (Albemarle Artillery),
    Capt. James W. Wyatt
    1 - 12-pdr howitzer   (100)   0-12-1
    2 – 3" rifles
    1 - 10-pdr Parrott

Reserve Artillery, Col. R. Lindsay Walker

Maj. David G. McIntosh's Battalion

Hurt's (Alabama) Battery, (Hardaway Artillery), Capt. William B. Hurt
    2 – 3" rifles   (75)   0-4-4
    2 - Whitworth rifles

Wallace's (Virginia) Battery, (2nd Rockbridge Artillery),
    Lt. Samuel Wallace
    2 - Napoleons   (71)   3-3-0
    2 – 3" rifles
Johnson's (Virginia) Battery, (Richmond Battery),
    Capt. Marmaduke Johnson
    4 – 3" rifles   (102)   5-1-4

Rice's (Virginia) Battery, (Danville Artillery), Capt. R. Sidney Rice
    4 - Napoleons   (121) 0-1-1

Maj. William J. Pegram's Battalion, Capt. Ervin B. Brunson

Brander's (Virginia) Battery, (Letcher Artillery),
    Capt. Thomas A. Brander
    2 - Napoleons (65)   3-11-3
    2 - 10-pdr Parrotts

Zimmerman's (South Carolina), Battery (Pee Dee Artillery),
    Lt. William E. Zimmerman
    4 – 3" rifles   (69)   1-?-?

Johnston's (Virginia) Battery, [W.G. Crenshaw's] (Richmond Battery),
    Lt. Andrew B. Johnston
    2 - 12-pdr howitzers   (81)   1-14-0
    2 – 3" rifles

McGraw's (Virginia) Battery, (Purcell Artillery), Capt. Joseph McGraw
    4 - Napoleons (95)   1-5-0

Marye's (Virginia) Battery, (Fredericksburg Artillery),
    Capt. Edward A. Marye
    2 - Napoleons (75)   2-0-0
    2 – 3" rifles

Stuart's Division Horse Artillery, Maj. Robert F. Beckham

Breathed's (Virginia) Battery, Capt. James Breathed
    4 – 3" rifles   (112)   0-1-0

Griffin's (Maryland) Battery, (2nd Baltimore Maryland Artillery),
    Capt. Willam H. Griffin
    4 - 10-pdr Parrotts   (112)   ?-?-?

McGregor's (Virginia) Battery, (2nd Stuart Horse Artillery),
    Capt. William M. McGregor
    2 - Napoleons (112)   0-0-2
    2 – 3" rifles

Hart's (South Carolina) Battery, (Washington Artillery),
    Capt. James F. Hart
    3 - Blakely rifles (113)   1-0-0

Chew's (Virginia) Battery, (Ashby Horse Artillery),
Capt. R. Preston Chew
1 - 3" rifle   (99)   ?-?-?
1 – 12-pdr howitzer

Moorman's (Virginia) Battery, (Beauregard Rifles),
Capt. Marcellus N. Moorman
1 - Napoleon   (112)   ?-?-?
3 - 3" rifles

Imboden's Command, Gen. John D. Imboden

McClanahan's (Virginia) Battery, (Staunton Horse Battery),
Capt. John H. McClanahan
4 - 12-pdr howitzers   (142)   ?-?-?
1 - 3" rifle

Jackson's (Virginia) Battery, (Charlottesville Horse Battery),
Capt. Thomas E. Jackson
2 - 12-pdr howitzers   (113)   ?-?-?
2 – 3" rifles
(*Assigned to Gen. Albert G. Jenkins' cavalry brigade at Gettysburg.*)

Total, Gettysburg Campaign
269-283 guns in 70 batteries
about 6,800 men, 4,100 horses,
566 limbers, 283 caissons,
70 travelling forge wagons and 70 battery wagons
Losses: (at Gettysburg)
94 killed, 437 wounded, 77 missing and prisoners, total 608

The Confederate Army captured from U.S. forces three 10-pdr Parrotts, one 3" rifle and three Napoleons. [13]

Type and Quantity of Guns at Gettysburg

Army of the Potomac

Napoleons	142
3" Ordnance Rifles	146
10-pdr. Parrotts	60
20-pdr. Parrotts	6
James Rifles	4
12-pdr. Howitzers	2
	360

Army of Northern Virginia

6pdr. Field Gun	1
12-pdr. Howitzers	26
Napoleons	107
24-pdr. Howitzers	4
3" Ordnance Rifles	73
3" Navy Rifles	4
Blakely Rifles	3
10-pdr. Parrotts	42
20-pdr. Parrotts	10
Whitworth Rifles	2
	272

In 1861 the U.S. Army had in its arsenal only 330 light field artillery guns. By 1865 the government had purchased 4,048 field guns, including 587 10-pounder Parrotts, 338 20-pounder Parrotts, 925 3-inch Ordnance Rifles, and 1,127 12-pounder Napoleons.

Gun	Tube made of	Caliber (inches)	Tube (lbs.)	Powder charge (lbs.)	Weight of projectile	Range (yards)	Types of ammunition used
Napoleon 12-pounder	bronze	4.62	1200	2.5	12 lbs.	1600 (canister 400)	solid shot, shell, spherical case, canister
Parrott Rifle 10-pounder	cast and wrought iron	3.00	900	1.0	9.5 lbs.	1850	shell, spherical case, canister
Parrott Rifle 20-pounder	cast and wrought iron	3.67	1800	2.0	20 lbs.	1900	shell, spherical case, canister
3-inch Ordnance Rifle	wrought iron	3.00	820-850	1.5	9.5 lbs.	1830	shell, spherical case, canister
Howitzer 12-pounder	bronze	4.62	788	1.25	10-12 lbs.	1070	shell, spherical case, canister
Howitzer 24-pounder	bronze	5.82	1318	2.5	18-24 lbs.	1100	shell, spherical case, canister
Whitworth Rifle	iron	2.75	1,100	1.75	12 lbs.	2800	solid "bolt," shell, spherical case, canister
James Rifle	bronze	3.67	875	0.75	12 lbs.	1700	shell, spherical case, canister
Blakely Rifle	iron	3.40	800	1.00	10 lbs.	1850	shell, spherical case, canister
Field Gun 6-pounder	bronze	3.67	884	1.25	4-6 lbs.	1500	shell, solid shot, spherical case, canister

Approximate figures. Calculated with 5 second time fuses, 5 degree elevation, and using case shot.
See: Peterson, *Round Shot and Rammers*, p. 96 and Gibbon, *The Artillerist's Manual*, Appendix pp. 40-42.

The Guns

and Their Ammunition

The artillery weapons employed by the two armies during the Gettysburg Campaign were generally of similar types and calibers, with the total number being at least 630 guns. Of these, 276 were smoothbores and 355 rifles. A complete breakdown of the artillery is as follows: The Union army had between 358 and 372 cannon, (depending on the source consulted), consisting of approximately 144 smoothbores and 218 rifles. There were reportedly, 144 3-inch Ordnance Rifles, 60 10-pounder Parrotts, six 20-pounder Parrotts, 142 12-pounder Napoleons, two 12-pounder Howitzers, and four James Rifles. The Confederate army carried with it somewhere between 269 and 283 guns, again sources vary, including one six-pounder field gun (bronze), 26 12-pounder Howitzers, four 24-pounder Howitzers, 101 12-pounder Napoleons, 80 3-inch Ordnance Rifles, 42 10-pounder Parrotts, ten 20-pounder Parrotts, three Blakely Rifles, and two Whitworth Rifles, in all, about 132 smoothbores and 137 rifled pieces.

The Napoleon, or 12-pounder smoothbore was a muzzle-loading bronze piece, (bronze was composed of 90 parts copper to 10 parts tin), which weighed approximately 1,200 pounds, and had a bore caliber of 4.62 inches. This cannon was theoretically capable, when using a charge of two and one-half pounds of black-powder, of hurling a 12-pound solid cannon ball or shot, somewhere between 1,500 and 1,700 yards. (A mile is 1,760 yards). This distance was achieved with the tube at an elevation of five  degrees. However, the Napoleon was seldom used over 1,200 yards when employing solid shot, shell, and spherical case, (i.e., shrapnel). When firing canister under 400 yards it was considered a very effective "anti-personnel" weapon against infantry assault formations. The muzzle velocity was 1,400 feet per second at the muzzle. The difference in a Southern or Northern manufactured Napoleon can be seen at a distance by noting the muzzle. The Confederate gun tube is straight and blunt, while the Union barrel has a pronounced sculptured "swell" or bulge at its mouth.

The 10-pounder Parrott Rifle was in the form of a cast-iron tube, interior cooled, and made more durable by the application of a reinforcing jacket of wrought iron shrunk around the breech. The tubes came in various sizes, with the more common 10-pounder and 20-

pounder in use at Gettysburg. The 10-pounder, with a 2.9-3.0 inch bore, weighed nearly 900 pounds, and was said to have a range of 5,000 yards at an elevation of 20 degrees, and 6,200 yards at an elevation of thirty-five degrees, using a standard one-pound load of black-powder. Its practical range was in fact, more between 2,400 and 3,000 yards. As the name implies, the projectile for this gun weighed about ten pounds.

The 20-pounder Parrotts and *3-inch Navy Rifles* straddled the fence between light field artillery and siege artillery. At 1,800 pounds, this weapon was almost too heavy for general use, especially considering that its effective range was only about that of the 10-pounder, at 2,800 yards. Together, Lee's and Meade's armies had no more than 16 of these in their arsenals. They were bored at 3.67 inches and took a charge of two pounds of powder, and the projectile weighed just under 20 pounds.

The 3-inch Ordnance Rifle with its long, sleek, slender barrel was constructed by wrapping boilerplate, (wrought-iron sheets) around a

mandrel. (the supporting bar on a lathe), and heating or welding it, and then rolling it into shape. This "ordnance gun" was the lightest in weight, at between 820 and 850 pounds. It used a one and one-half pound black-powder charge in its three-inch diameter bore. Again, theoretically it had nearly a 4,000-yard range, but in actuality this gun was not often fired in combat out to more than 2,500-2,800 yards.

A *Howitzer* was a bronze gun with a tapered powder chamber at the base of the barrel. This allowed the use of lighter powder charges. Designed to fire at shorter ranges with higher trajectories, howitzers were made in various sizes. Twelve and 24-pounders can be found at Gettysburg. The barrels appear "stubbier" than the more common Napoleons, and do not have that cannon's characteristic swell at the muzzle. About two dozen were present at Gettysburg, all with the Army of Northern Virginia.

The Whitworth Rifle was a breechloading gun, produced in England, with a 2.75-inch hexagonal bore. The iron barrel weighed 1,100 pounds, fired a 10-pound projectile, and was capable of a range in excess of 5,000 yards, but realistically 2,500 yards was more effective, and near the average under battle conditions. Two Whitworths accompanied the Confederate Army into Pennsylvania in 1863.

Four other artillery types were part of the ordnance makeup at the Battle of Gettysburg. Cast iron *Brooke Rifles,* for one, developed by the Confederate States, were similar in construction and characteristics to the U.S. Parrott rifle.

The James Rifle was made of cast bronze, with a caliber of 3.67 inches and a weight of 875 pounds. The charge was 0.75 pounds of black-powder used to throw a 12-pound projectile 1,700 yards. This was the only bronze cannon which had a rifled bore, which employed 15 lands and grooves. (See photograph on page 37.)

Three *Blakely 12-pounder* guns were present with Gen. J.E.B. Stuart's Confederate cavalry; like the Whitworths these guns had been run through the Federal blockade from England. With a 2.5-inch rifled bore and a 1.5-pound powder charge, a Blakely was capable of ranges up to 2,000 yards with very good accuracy. Reportedly, they "kicked like a mule," and often damaged their own carriages by this hard recoil.

Only one *smoothbore 6-pounder* Field Gun was present on the battlefield of Gettysburg. It came North with Lee's army attached to a North Carolina battery, and claimed a range of 1,500 yards when using 1.25 pounds of powder. The 6-pounder's bronze tube weighed in at 884 pounds and its bore diameter was 3.67 inches.

Ammunition

All field artillery guns went into action with four ammunition chests, mounted onto the limbers and caisson of each piece. These wooden and metal-trimmed boxes could transport four types of rounds: solid shot, shell, spherical case shot or shrapnel, and canister.

Solid Shot was a solid projectile used primarily for demolition and ricochet fire. It was recommended for ranges over 350 yards, and was often used against infantry or opposing artillery batteries at 1,000 yards or more, and against cavalry at 1,200 yards if the ground was favorable.

A *Shell* was a hollow, cast-iron projectile, ¾ of an inch thick, fitted with a fuse, and filled with a bursting charge (seven or eight ounces) of

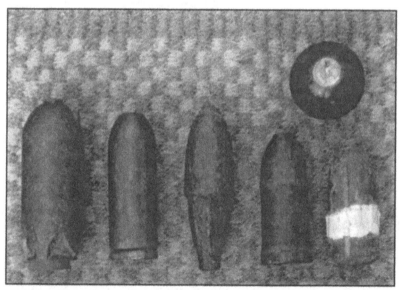

A variety of common projectiles used at Gettysburg. From left to right, they are: 20-pounder Parrott, 10-pounder Parrott, 3-inch Schenkl, C.S. Read, 3-inch Hotchkiss, and (top) 12-pounder spherical shell.

granulated black-powder, which upon detonation broke the shell casing and scattered usually four or five iron fragments in several directions. Rifled guns used cylindro-conoidal shaped projectiles, while smoothbore cannons employed the spherical shaped type.

When fired at a target, it could be somewhat effective, depending on the range, the competency of the gun crew, the type of terrain, weather conditions, and the quality of the fuses in use. It was fired less against infantry than case shot, (shrapnel) or canister, and the fuse could be timed to burst from 0 to 5 seconds. At an elevation of three degrees and 75 seconds (3,600 seconds = 1 degree), a range of 1,300 yards might be attained.

Spherical Case Shot or Shrapnel rounds were similar to shells in that they were hollow, cast-iron containers. But unlike a shell, case shot was filled with round musket balls or other types of "shrapnel," (named after British Gen. Henry Shrapnel who invented it), which was sealed with melted resin. A hole drilled into this matrix of lead balls held sufficient powder to rupture the outer case, which, when it exploded, threw the balls and iron fragments out in a destructive 360-degree pattern. The projectile used to momentum of its flight through the air, and not simply the bursting charge, to give the shrapnel the ability to cause injury or death. Several fuses could be affixed before loading, and the safety limit from the muzzle was a range greater

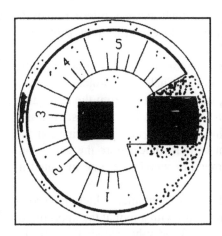 

View of a 12-pounder spherical case shot, showing the Bormann time fuse, the lead shrapnel balls contained in the sulfur "matrix", and the bursting charge running into the center of the shell. At left is a detailed illustration of a Bormann time fuse.

than 500 yards. Shrapnel or case was primarily an anti-personnel round for use beyond canister range, and was normally fused to explode fifty to seventy-five yards in front of the target and fifteen to twenty yards above it.

The *Canister* round was primarily a defensive type of ammunition, fired mainly at targets under 400 yards, and was considered the only really effective cannon projectile in use against infantry during the Civil War. It turned a field piece into a giant shotgun. Very simply made, canister consisted of a tin cylinder filled with cast-iron or lead shot packed in tiers, with a sawdust filler. In most cases, between 27 and 50 shot were contained in field artillery canister rounds. Below 150 yards, double canister, or two of the tin cylinders could be fired into an attacking enemy's line or column. "*Grape*," which consisted of larger iron balls fastened around a core of wood or metal in three tiers of nine, resembled a grape cluster, and was not often utilized in Civil War field guns. Its effective range was anywhere up to 800 yards. The United States had discontinued it before the war; however the Confederate army periodically employed "grape" in a small number of their field artillery batteries.

Fuses

Fuses are the detonating devices which cause artillery rounds to explode. There were several types of fuses utilized in projectiles during the years between 1861-1865.

Time Fuses. This two-pronged system, the most common variety, was designed to detonate a case shot or shell type projectile after a predetermined number of seconds, using the flame from the exploding powder charge in the cannon barrel to ignite it. The first system was a powder composition, wrapped tightly in paper, and pre-divined at the factory to insure a specific amount of burn time before the explosion. The paper fuse was driven into a metal or wood fuse plug mounted in the fuse hole of the projectile.

A second system used a soft metal container which housed a powder train. The cannoneer cut this train with a tool at the appropriate time mark before loading. "Bormann" fused spherical shells were the most common rounds engaging these methods.

Percussion Fuse. This was the second most utilized system, and was designed to burst a shell projectile when the fuse struck an object. Most styles employed a plunger-and-anvil method of detonation. The body of the fuse was made of brass, copper, or alloy and was screwed into the nose of the projectile. Upon hitting the target, a striker was driven down a chamber inside the fuse where it hit a percussion cap. When the cap exploded it ignited the powder train which then burned down into the powder chamber and blew up the projectile. The normal rounds using the percussion fuse were the Parrott, Hotchkiss, James, and Schenkl.

Combination Fuse. This system was a composite of both time and percussion fuses and, depending on the manufacturer, was widely varied in its method of setting off the bursting charge in case shot projectiles. Basically, the fuse was set prior to firing to an exact detonation time, and was activated by the inertia of the shock in being blown from the cannon tube. This "firing shock" caused a plunger to slide down and strike a chemical-composition against a metal shelf, which started a flame that ignited the powder train. However, if the projectile struck an object before the time element was completed, the system was designed to act as a percussion fuse. [14]

The first Union cannon shot at Gettysburg was fired on July 1 by a 3-inch Ordnance Rifle [Tube #233] in Lt. John Calef's Battery A, 2ⁿᵈ U.S. Artillery on McPherson's Ridge. That original gun tube can be seen today on the same sight, at the base of Gen. John Buford.

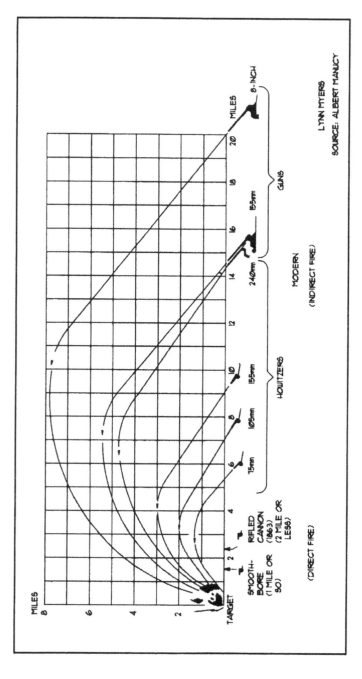

This diagram illustrates the differences between Civil War and modern artillery. An 1860s era cannon had to fire directly at a target much like a soldier fires a weapon from his shoulder, and ranges were very limited. However, 20th and 21st century guns and howitzers can now obtain extreme accuracy and distances. While battles between 1861-1865 experienced artillery casualties at usually less than 10%; newer cannons are capable of inflicting losses of 75% or higher.

Glossary

Artificer — this was essentially the blacksmith or mechanic for a battery. They made all repairs to the carriages and weapons, as well as shoeing the horses.

Breech — the back end of the gun barrel.

Breechblock — a movable piece which closed the breech of a cannon, as in the British Whitworth gun. The majority of Civil War cannons were, however, muzzle-loading weapons.

Bursting charge — The small powder charge used to detonate shell or case shot.

Caisson — the two-wheeled ammunition carriage which accompanied a fieldpiece. It was transported by a limber and four to six horses, and was made up of two ammunition chests and carried a spare wheel.

Cascabel — the knob of a cannon at the end of the breech.

Deviation — The variations in the trajectories of like projectiles fired under the same conditions.

Drift — The left or right deviation of a projectile from its intended path.

En echelon — a step-like formation of units, in which each unit is progressively to the left or right of the one preceding it. A subdivision of a combat force, as an assault *en echelon*, whereby units advanced slightly ahead or behind the troops to the left or right.

Enfilade — to rake with fire. Gunfire directed from either flank along the length of a column or line of troops. It can also be a disposition or placement of troops that makes them vulnerable to such fire.

Field artillery — Weapons small enough to maneuver through difficult terrain and light enough to keep up with a moving army and its rapid changes.

Friction primer — a device used to fire cannons It consisted of two small brass tubes soldered at right angles to each other. The longer tube was filled with rifle-powder, and was inserted into the vent at the breech of the cannon. The upper, shorter tube contained fine-grained friction powder, and through its center ran a piece of wire with serrated edges. The other end of the wire was twisted into the form of a loop through which the lanyard hook was attached. To fire the cannon, the lanyard was pulled which brought the burred end of the wire through the fine powder igniting it, which in turn lit the rifle-powder. This small, directed charge then exploded down into the powder bag that sat behind the projectile inside the gun tube, setting off the piece.

Gunpowder — a composition of saltpeter (76 parts), charcoal (14 parts), and sulfur (10 parts). The charcoal is the combustible part, while the saltpeter furnishes the oxygen, and changes the mass into gas; the sulfur gives intensity of heat.

Handspike — a wooden "lever," when fitted into the "pointing" rings on the end the carriage trail was used to turn and point the gun.

Howitzer — A short-barreled artillery piece used primarily for firing hollow projectiles. It had a powder chamber in the rear of the barrel with a diameter smaller than that of the bore.

Initial velocity — The speed of the projectile when it left the barrel.

Lanyard — a thin rope with a wooden handle at one end and a small hook on the other. The hook was attached to the friction primer and when pulled, fired the cannon.

Lay — to aim a gun.

Limber — a two-wheeled vehicle, pulled by horses, to which the gun trail was attached for transport. The limber carried one ammunition chest that could hold about 50 rounds. It also conveyed the caisson.

Lunette — small earthwork often dug to give the gunners some protection. The walls were usually braced by a log barricade. Also the circular grommet at the rear of the cannon carriage trail.

Muzzle — the front end of the gun barrel through which the ball is loaded and fired.

Prolonge, firing by — a method by which an artillery piece could be moved or retired while still directing shots at an advancing enemy force. A "prolonge" rope was attached to the gun and then to the limber. As the piece recoiled in the act of discharge, the gun was dragged backward with the rope by its limber to the rear, while the gunners continued to load and fire at will.

Rammer/Sponge — A wooden staff with a head to force the powder charge and projectile into the barrel. The sponge, on the opposite end, was to swab out the gun, extinguishing burning embers from the previous shot.

Range — the horizontal distance from a gun to its target or to the point where the projectile first hits the ground. Effective range was the distance at which effective results could be expected, and was usually not the same as maximum range, which means the extreme limit of range.

Ricochet — the rebounding of a shot, usually propelled by a small charge, and with the gun pointed at an elevation of less than 10 degrees. By striking in more spots than one, like a stone skipping over the surface of a pond, the projectile could do greater damage.

Rotating band — a band of soft metal, such as copper, brass, or lead, which encircled the projectile. By tightly engaging the bands of the spiral rifling in the bore, the band caused rotation of the projectile.

Rotating bands for muzzle-loading cannon were expansion rings, and the powder blast expanded the ring into the rifling grooves.

Section — two guns of a six or four gun battery, usually commanded by a lieutenant.

Spike — to close the vent of a gun with a nail forcibly driven in, so as to render it temporarily useless. Guns were spiked when they were in danger of falling into enemy hands.

Vent — a small opening in the top of the breech of the cannon barrel into which the friction primer was placed in order to fire the piece.

Volley — the simultaneous discharge of a number of cannon.

Windage — the difference between the diameter of the shot and the diameter of the bore.[15]

Notes

1. Bates, Samuel P. *History of Pennsylvania Volunteers, 1861-1865* (Harrisburg, PA: 1869-71), 1229.

2. Spangler, Edward W. *My Little War Experience* (York, PA: 1904), 37.

3. Small, Sam. *The Horse Soldier Catalog.* Vol. 23, (Gettysburg, PA: Winter, 1996), Vol. 23, 50-51.

4. Campbell, Eric. "Baptism of Fire: The Ninth Massachusetts Battery at Gettysburg, July 2, 1863," *Gettysburg*, Vol. 5 (Dayton, OH: July 1991), 71-72.

5. Venn, Frank H. "That Flag of Truce at Antietam," *Confederate Veteran*, Vol. IV (Nashville, TN: 1896), 389.

6. Burpee, Lt. Edgar A., Unpublished letter dated July 12, 1863, in the collection of Len Rosa, Gettysburg, PA and used with his permission. Carter, Robert G., *Four Brothers in Blue* (Austin, TX: 1978), 324-325.

7. Wert, John H., *A Complete Hand-book of the Monuments and Dedications on the Gettysburg Battlefield* (Harrisburg, PA:1886), 109

8. Janes, Henry, M.D., Letter published in the Baltimore *Sun*, Oct. 27, 1899.

9. Griffith, Paddy. *Battle Tactics of the Civil War* (New Haven, CT: 1989), 177-178.

10. Scott, John K.P. His original manuscript written c.1890 and now in the author's private collection. It was paraphrased and heavily edited as a general outline for the narrative sections of this book. The only known publication of his history is in the form of an unknown and undated newspaper article present in the library of the G.N.M.P. U.S. Government, *Official Records of the War of the Rebellion,* Vol. 27, Parts I & II (Washington, DC: 1889). Hereafter cited as *OR.* Longstreet, James. "Lee in Pennsylvania," *The Annals of the War* (Dayton, OH: Morningside Press, 1988), 429-430. Longstreet, James, "The Mistakes of Gettysburg," *The Annals of the War,* 631-632.

11. Ibid.

12. Downey, Fairfax. *The Guns at Gettysburg* (New York: 1958). *OR*, Vol. 27, Part I, 155-168. *OR.* Vol. 27, Part I, 173-187. Busey, John W. & David G. Martin. *Regimental Strengths and Losses at Gettysburg* (Hightstown, NJ: 1994, 59-117, 129-201, 233-234.

13. Downey, Fairfax. *The Guns at Gettysburg. OR,* Vol. 27, Part II, 283-292. Crute, Joseph H. Jr., *Units of the Confederate States Army* (Midlothian, VA: 1987). *OR,.* Vol. 27, Part II, 329-346. Busey & Martin, 59-117, 129-201, 233-234.

14. Coggins, Jack, *Arms and Equipment of the Civil War* (Wilmington, NC: 1987), 63-85. Thomas, Dean S., *Cannons* (Gettysburg, PA: 1985.) Peterson, Harold L., *Round Shot and Rammers* (New York: 1969). 88-96. Ripley, Warren, *Artillery and Ammunition of the Civil War* (New York: 1970), 17-45, 109-115, 255-345. Melton, Jack W. Jr. and L. E. Pawl, *Introduction to Field Artillery Ordnance, 1861-1865* (Kennesaw, GA: 1994), 38-39.

15. Ripley,. 353-355. Manucy, Albert. *Artillery Through the Ages.* (Washington, DC: 1949), 87-88.

Greg Coco speaking with servicemen in the Gettysburg National Military Park Soldiers' National Cemetery on July 19, 2005 *(Katie Lawhon, NPS)*.

About the Author

Gregory Ashton Coco, born and raised in Louisiana, lived in the Gettysburg area for nearly 35 years.

In 1972, after serving in the U.S. Army, he earned a degree in American History from the University of Southwestern Louisiana. While in the military, Greg spent a tour of duty in Vietnam as a prisoner of war military interrogator and infantry platoon radio operator with the 25th Infantry and received, among other awards, the Purple Heart and Bronze Star.

During his years in Gettysburg, Greg worked as a National Park Service Ranger and a Licensed Battlefield Guide. He wrote sixteen books and a dozen scholarly articles on Gettysburg and the Civil War. His book *A Strange and Blighted Land. Gettysburg: The Aftermath of a Battle* was voted #12 in the Top 50 Civil War Books ever written.

Greg died at age 62 in February of 2009. In his words, he was "the happy husband of Cindy L. Small for 26 years. He was the fortunate father of daughter Keri E. Coco. He loved them both with all his heart." Keri is married to Cail MacLean and they have a daughter, Ashton MacLean Coco.